H KAINH

ΔΙΑΘΗΚΗ.

NOVUM

TESTAMENTUM.

JUXTA EXEMPLAR JOANNIS MILLII AC-
CURATISSIME IMPRESSUM.

EDITIO PRIMA AMERICANA.

WIGORNIÆ, MASSACHUSETTENSI :
Excudebat ISAIAS THOMAS, Jun.
SINGULATIM ET NUMEROSE EO VENDITA OFFICINA SUA,
APRIL—1800.

The First Greek Testament Printed in America. Facsimile of Title.
Full size.

μνησθητε των ρημάτων των
προειρημένων ὑπὸ των ἀποσ-
τόλων τῦ Κυρίε ἡμῶν Ἰησοῦ
Χρισοῦ·

18 Ὅτι ἔλεγον ὑμῖν, ὅτι
ἐν ἐσχάτῳ χρόνῳ ἔσονται ἐμ-
παῖκται, κατὰ τὰς ἑαυτῶν ἐπ-
ιθυμίας πορευόμενοι τῶν ἀσε-
βειῶν.

19 Οὗτοί εἰσιν οἱ ἀποδι-
ορίζοντες ἑαυτοὺς, ψυχικοὶ,
πνεῦμα μὴ ἔχοντες.

20 Ὑμεῖς δὲ, ἀγαπητοὶ,
τῇ ἁγιωτάτῃ ὑμῶν πίστει ἐπ-
οικοδομῦντες ἑαυτὺς, ἐν Πνεύ-
ματι ἁγίῳ προσευχόμενοι,

21 Ἑαυτὺς ἐν ἀγάπῃ Θεῦ
τηρήσατε, προσδεχόμενοι τὰ

ἔλεος τῦ Κυρίε ὑμῶν Ἰησῦ
Χρισοῦ εἰς ζωὴν αἰώνιαν.

22 Καὶ ὃς μὲν ἐλεεῖτε
διακρινόμενοι·

23 Οὓς δὲ ἐν φόβῳ σώ-
ζετε, ἐκ τοῦ πυρὸς ἁρπάζον-
τες, μισοῦντες κ̀ τὸν ἀπὸ τῆς
σαρκὸς ἐσπιλωμένον χιτῶνα.

24 Τῷ δὲ δυναμένῳ φυ-
λάξαι ὑμᾶς ἀπταίσυς, κ̀ σῆ-
σαι κατενώπιον τῆς δόξης αὐτῦ ἀμώμυς ἐν ἀγαλλιάσει,

25 Μόνῳ Σοφῷ Θεῷ Σω-
τῆρι ἡμῶν δόξα κ̀ μεγαλωσύ-
νη, κράτος κ̀ ἐξυσία, κ̀ νῦν κ̀
εἰς πάντας τὺς αἰῶνας. Ἀμήν.

Ἐπιστολὴ Ἰύδα καθολικὴ
στίχων οδ.

ΑΠΟΚΑΛΥΨΙΣ ΙΩΑΝΝΟΥ

ΤΟΥ ΘΕΟΛΟΓΟΥ.

Κεφ. ά. 1.

ΑΠΟΚΑΛΥΨΙΣ Ἰη-
σοῦ Χρισοῦ, ἣν ἔδωκεν
αὐτῷ ὁ Θεὸς, δεῖξαι τοῖς δύ-
λοις αὐτῦ ἃ δεῖ γενέσθαι ἐν
τάχει· κ̀ ἐσήμανεν ἀποστείλας
διὰ τῦ ἀγγέλε αὐτῦ τῷ δύλῳ
αὐτῦ Ἰωάννῃ·

2 Ὃς ἐμαρτύρησε τὸν λό-
γον τῦ Θεῦ, κ̀ τὴν μαρτυρίαν
Ἰησοῦ Χρισοῦ, ὅσα τε εἶδε.

3 Μακάριος ὁ ἀναγινώσ-
κων, κ̀ οἱ ἀκύοντες τὺς λόγυς
τῆς προφητείας, κ̀ τηροῦντες

τὰ ἐν αὐτῇ γεγραμμένα· ὁ
γὰρ καιρὸς ἐγγύς.

4 Ἰωάννης ταῖς ἑπτὰ ἐκ-
κλησίαις ταῖς ἐν τῇ Ἀσίᾳ.
χάρις ὑμῖν κ̀ εἰρήνη ἀπὸ τῦ
ὁ ὢν κ̀ ὁ ἦν κ̀ ὁ ἐρχόμενος·
κ̀ ἀπὸ τῶν ἑπτὰ πνευμάτων
ἃ ἐστιν ἐνώπιον τῦ θρόνε αὐτῦ,

5 Καὶ ἀπὸ Ἰησοῦ Χρισοῦ
ὁ μάρτυς ὁ πιστὸς, ὁ πρωτότο-
κος ἐκ τῶν νεκρῶν, κ̀ ὁ ἄρ-
χων τῶν βασιλέων τῆς γῆς.
τῷ ἀγαπήσαντι ἡμᾶς, κ̀ λύ-
σαντι ἡμᾶς ἀπὸ τῶν ἁμαρτι-
ῶν

The First Greek Testament Printed in America. Facsimile of text, page 448,
Jude 17 to Rev. 1 : 5, showing most of the varieties of type employed, and the
misprint in Jude 25. Full size.

A

CRITICAL BIBLIOGRAPHY

OF THE

GREEK NEW TESTAMENT

AS

PUBLISHED IN AMERICA

BY

ISAAC H HALL A M LL B Pʜ D

WITH TWO FACSIMILE ILLUSTRATIONS

WIPF & STOCK · Eugene, Oregon

Wipf and Stock Publishers
199 W 8th Ave, Suite 3
Eugene, OR 97401

American Greek Testaments. A Critical Bibliography of
the Greek New Testament, as Published in America
By Hall, Isaac H.
ISBN 13: 978-1-60899-609-4
Publication date 4/5/2010
Previously published by PIckwich and Co., 1883

PREFACE.

THE present work, as the reader will perceive, is but one branch, and an indirect outcome, of long research in a more comprehensive field of study. But, that branch once taken up, it has been explored with all possible thoroughness; and wherever the present investigation has found its limit, an attempt is made to indicate the twigs upon which fruit may still be hanging out of reach.

Bibliographic work, according to all experience, is never perfect. Diligence along the lines of regular information and of systematic search is ever supplemented by the knowledge that comes only by chance. The antiquarian bookstore, the street stall, or the rag-dealer's stock, will now and then reveal a series of facts to which the librarians, the publishers, or the bibliophiles, could give no clue. Fortune is said proverbially to favor the collector and the bibliographer; but the latter knows that she distributes her favors, and bestows all upon none. He must be content with doing his best; and, after exhausting the obvious sources of information, and following up the obscurer clues, he must be willing to put his results into permanent form without waiting too long for mere windfalls.

The original groundwork of the following pages is a paper on The Greek New Testament as Published in America, presented to the American Philological Association at its meeting in Cambridge in 1882, and published in their transactions for that year. The wide distribution of that essay opened many new sources of information hitherto inaccessible or undiscovered, furnishing data for the addition of many items, besides a few corrections. It brought the author into communication with persons whom he had supposed to be no longer living, and thus rescued not a few facts from irrecoverable uncertainty or speedy oblivion. The quantity of information thus gained—adding well nigh a hundred to the number of books enumerated, and putting a different aspect upon sundry historical matters—together with the flattering reception which that paper met with on both sides of the Atlantic, seemed to make the way clear for a more complete presentation of the subject.

In the former publication, the author depended almost entirely upon his personal inspection of books, and his single-handed research; and these are still the basis of by far the greater portion of the following statements. But in completing the present work, he has many to thank for information kindly communicated, often at the expense of no little trouble and research. Help has been furnished unsparingly, and even with enthusiasm. To mention all to whom the author is indebted, either for positive additions of fact, or for aid in sifting contradictory testimony and ascertaining the truth about matters heretofore in dispute or doubt, is out of the question here; but the author's thanks to each are none the less sincere and particular. The publishers, the librarians, and the scholars, have responded with cheerful readiness to requests which sometimes even bordered on the unreasonable. It would be unjust, however, to omit special mention of the unusual kindness and efficiency of Dr. Ezra Abbot, of Cambridge, and Dr. Benjamin B. Warfield, of Allegheny, the former for supplying difficult and elusive items of divers sorts, and the latter in pointing out more than a score of issues of the Greek New Testament that were omitted in the former publication. To a few librarians letters of inquiry have been posted, from whom no reply has come. But more than two of these pages would be occupied with a list of those whose kind responses to the writer's inquiries have been more free, more full, and more painstaking, than he had dared to ask.

Personal verification, however, where possible, has never been neglected, whatever may have been the source or the means of new information; and no pains have been spared to secure accuracy. If any slip or omission is discovered, the author will be grateful to any one who shall make it known to him.

PHILADELPHIA, October, 1883.

GREEK NEW TESTAMENT

AS

PUBLISHED IN AMERICA.

I. PRELIMINARY.

ASIDE from the bibliophile's passion or the collector's mania, there are sundry sound reasons for an inquiry into the history and character of the Greek New Testament as published in America. Most of these reasons are those developed by the inquiry itself, and centre themselves in the varieties of text thus disclosed; varieties existing not only in the critical editions, but in the adored *textus receptus* itself—before the critical editions had much circulation, or, as to most of them, an existence. The critic, no less than the bibliographer, has an interest in the investigation.

Secondary, but still a fact and noteworthy, is the revelation thus made of the industry and enthusiasm of the earlier American editors,; who, to a greater extent than is commonly suspected, exercised an independent judgment and skill. Although their pioneer work would not fill the wants of to-day, it has been rather too meanly judged by their successors, and deserves at least an honorable record.

The ground, moreover, is almost unbroken. In O'Callaghan's American Bibles,[1] only sixteen editions of the Greek Testament are described or enumerated; a mere fraction of the number then existing; not to mention those issued in the twenty-three years that have since elapsed—nearly all of them prolific, except the four years of war.

---

[1] A List of Editions of the Holy Scriptures and Parts thereof, printed in America previous to 1860. By E. B. O'Callaghan. Albany, 1861.

In the last two centuries, though theological books abounded, it was an almost unheard of thing to see a quotation from the Greek Testament—at least, in Greek type—in an American book. Nor were the English citations always made from our Common Version. The lawyers were apt to follow Coke's example, or to cite at second hand from him and others, who quoted the Vulgate Latin and supplied an original rendering therefrom. The clergymen had not altogether ceased to use or to quote the Genevan Bible, the version which came over to New England with the early settlers, and which still is often to be seen preserved for its associations and its ancient family record.[1] To this day certain theological books are printed in this country with their Scripture citations from an English version earlier than our Common one. An every-day example of this is the edition of Luther's Commentary on Galatians commonly circulated among the Presbyterians. This translation (it is a revision as well) antedates our Common Version, and still keeps its Scripture citations unchanged.

Of course the Greek Testament was in the land, in numbers abundant for the times. I have no data, even approximate, to form a judgment as to the particular editions which were most common; but in the theological libraries and in private collections I have seen evidence of their great variety.[2] For many years, too, I have known it as a fact that the rarer and more highly prized editions used to be regularly sought by certain second-hand dealers for exportation to Europe; where, until recently, such old treasures readily brought a higher price than here. To judge from such facts as are apparent, the earlier immigrants chiefly brought editions produced in

[1] Most of these immigrant copies were printed just at the close of the sixteenth century, and contain as their New Testament portion that "Englished by L. Tomson," from the Latin of Theodore Beza.

[2] Of the 114 editions known to have been printed in the 16th century, I know of at least 60 in America (39 in my own library). About the same number were printed in the 17th century, and of these I know where to find more than 70 in America (39 in my own library). The proportions are much larger for the 18th and 19th centuries. I have made no special search for ancient editions possessed in this country; but I know that nearly, if not quite, all the important historical editions are to be found here; most of them more frequently than would be expected.

Antwerp, Leyden, Geneva, and Lyons, with a sprinkling from presses along the Rhine, and some of Paris make; but just before and after the American Revolution, more copies came from England and Scotland. However, but few editions were produced in England before the settlement of Massachusetts. I can find traces of but two[1] printed before 1620.

[1] These were Vautroller's (H. Stephens's text), London, 1587, 16mo; and another of the same text, *e Regia Typographia*, London, 1592, 16mo. The London Beza of 1565, mentioned by Scrivener (*Plain Introd. to N. T. Crit.*, ed. 1874, p. 390, note 1; also, his *N. T. Gr.*, ed. 1873, p. viii.) is doubtless a mistake, which is only made worse by its reiteration with fresh errors, in the 3d ed. of his *Plain Introd.* (1883), p. 440, note 2. The readings which Scrivener gives in the earlier edd. of his N. T. Gr. as those of " Bezæ 1565 " are not those of a genuine Beza. A like remark applies to his " Result of a Collation in the Apocalypse of Beza 1565 with St. and Elz." in his *Plain Introduction*, ed. of 1861, p. 311. He must have used a book which presented very nearly the text of *Henry Stephens.*

II. THE MILL EDITIONS.

THE earliest Greek *book*[1] printed in America, so far as I can discover, is the Enchiridion of Epictetus (" ex editione Joannis Upton accurate expressum "), with a Latin translation, published at Philadelphia by Mathew Carey in 1792 (some copies are dated 1793). The type is quite small, and is apparently the same as that used thirty years later, with much less skill, in Kneeland's Greek Testament—to be described farther on.

But the first Greek Testament printed in America, as all acquainted with the general subject know, was published at Worcester, Massachusetts, in 1800, by the famous printer Isaiah Thomas (b. 1749, d. 1831). The book is now rather uncommon, though easy enough to be had a few years ago.[2]

---

[1] In Isaiah Thomas's *History of Printing*, vol. I., pp. 251, 252, I find the following : "About the year 1718, when mr. Thomas Hollis, of London, a great benefactor to the college, among other gifts presented to the University a fount, or cast, of Hebrew, and another of Greek types, both of them were of the size of long primer. The Greek was not used till 1761, when the government of the college had a work printed, entitled, *Pietas et Gratulatio Collegii Cantabrigiensis apud Novanglos*, dedicated to King George the third, on his accession to the throne ; two of these poetical essays being written in Greek, called these types into use. They were never used but at that time, and were, in January, 1764, destroyed by the fire that consumed Harvard hall, one of the college buildings in which the types and college library were deposited ; the cast of Hebrew escaped, having been sent to Boston some time before, to print Sewall's Hebrew Grammar." The *Pietas et Gratulatio* was a magnificent 4to of 116 pages, consisting of thirty-one pieces (prize compositions, etc.) of various character, of which No. 15 was an 'ΕΛΕΓΕΙΟΝ, and No. 16 an 'ΩιΔΗ', both by Stephen Sewall ; and No. 18 an 'ΕΠΙΤΑΦΙΟΝ, by Governor Bernard. It was published under a vote of the Corporation, of Jan. 5, 1762, at Boston, by J. Green and J. Russell, and dated 1761. For full information respecting the work and a description of extant copies, see Justin Winsor's account in *Bulletin of the Library of Harvard University*, March, 1879 ; also a reprint of the same in *Bibliographical Contributions* No. 4, 1879.

[2] This edition appears to have been in very extensive use among the young stu-

8

It bears many slight resemblances to the various English editions of William Bowyer—a series of at least twelve editions, varying slightly one from another, which appeared in London at various times from 1715 to 1812. Of these Bowyer editions, that of 1794 (an edition not noticed by the bibliographers, but apparently the last of the series to appear before Thomas published) seems to have furnished Thomas with his title-pattern. At least, its title is exactly reproduced, line for line, word for word, and style for style of type, in the Thomas edition, except only as to date and names and place of publisher. Thomas's titlepage reads as follows: "H ΚΑΙΝΗ | ΔΙΑΘΗΚΗ. | NOVUM | TESTAMENTUM. | JUXTA EXEMPLAR JOANNIS MILLII AC- | CURATISSIME IMPRESSUM. | [Ornament—a caduceus with cornucopias at the sides.] | *EDITIO PRIMA AMERICANA.* | WIGORNIÆ MASSACHUSETTENSI: | Excudebat ISAIAS THOMAS, JUN. | SINGULATIM ET NUMEROSE EO VENDITA OFFICINÆ SUÆ, | APRIL — 1800." The book is a 12mo, pp. 478. Its titlepage and a specimen page of the text (Jude 17– Rev. 1 : 5) are given in facsimile in the two illustrations of the double frontispiece.

At the end of some copies is bound in a leaf of advertisements dated December 25, 1802; but the copies are all one impression; for stereotyping was then unknown in America, and no reason could exist for dating back the issue. The text is, of course, divided into verse-paragraphs. As to accessory matter, it has only one page, containing "A Chronological Table of the Books of the New Testament," with a statement at its end that it has "been, carefully and faithfully, collected from the writings of the famous Rev. Nathaniel Lardner, D.D." (The name Nathanael is here misspelled.) This table is signed "Caleb Alexander;" but no other external professions of editorship appear. A somewhat similar table, con-

dents and the literary men. I have talked with a number of people who in their boyhood knew no other edition. Chancellor Kent's copy, which is in my possession, has his autograph and the date 1807 written on the titlepage, and on a flyleaf a reference to the "M. Anthology" for January, 1808, for "an account of *Griesbach's* Edit. of the New Testament, and the History of the common Elzevir Text." This copy never was perfect, pp. 73–84 (1 sheet) and pp. 449-452 (2 leaves) having been omitted in the binding.

densed and altered from Mill and J. A. Fabricius, occupies a
like place in the Bowyer of 1794, and seems to have given
more than one hint for the construction of Alexander's table;
though the two differ slightly in length and in dates.   The
subscriptions to the Epistles copy those of Bowyer (or Mill
at second hand) exactly, even to giving the numbers of the
στίχοι in the various books (see the authorities therefor in
Küster's Mill), and that partly in Greek numerals and partly
in Greek words, just exactly as Mill and Bowyer gave them—
with only one difference.   That difference is, that these numbers are wanting in the subscriptions to 2 Corinthians, Galatians, 1 Thessalonians, and Titus; evidently because in each
of these cases one of the Greek numerals was the *koppa* or
sampi;[1] characters for which Thomas probably had no type,
nor an editor bold enough to spell out the numbers in words.

However, this edition does not appear to be a slavish reprint of any former work.   On the titlepage, to be sure, it
professes to be an accurate reprint of Mill; but so do many
other editions that exhibit intentional alterations.   The same
is true of the great majority of the very numerous English
editions which have made that profession—ever since the
original Mill appeared.   I have devoted no little time to
searching for some edition of which this one of Thomas
might be an exact reprint; but thus far I only find that
while some of the Bowyer editions show some of the same
alterations of Mill, no one of them agrees nearly enough
to pass for the exact pattern.   I must therefore believe
that the editor exercised his own judgment, and derived
his changes in the text from some edition of the Elzevir
family.

In order to show this, it must be remembered that three
leading editions were the main sources of the text of the
ordinary editions of that time.   These were Robert Stephens's of 1550, Beza's of 1565, and the Elzevir of 1678[2]

---

[1] In several of the Bowyer editions, including that of 1794, these characters
are replaced by *Hebrew* letters.

[2] The Elzevir editions of 1656, 1662, 1670, and 1678 are considerably smaller,
if not neater, than the preceding editions of 1624, 1633, and 1641, though less
sought by collectors.   They all correct the omission (in the editions of 1624,

(not of 1624 or 1633, though these are commonly regarded
as standards of comparison). Mill's edition (Oxford, 1707,
fol., and Küster's Mill with additions, Amsterdam and Rot-
terdam, 1710, Leipzig, 1723, 1746) keeps generally the text
of Stephanus, departing from it in only a few places of moment; such as Matt. 24 : 15, reading ἑστώς for ἑστός; 1 Pet.
3 : 11, adding ἀγαθόν· ζητησάτω; 1 Pet. 3 : 21, ᾧ καὶ ἡμᾶς for
ὃ καὶ ἡμᾶς; and Rev. 2 : 5, ταχὺ for τάχει. The Küster edition, indeed, returns to the Stephanic text in the first and last
of these places. Thus the Mill text might be classified as a
Stephanic text; and such would be its classification here, did
not a series of facts occur which compel a little different
treatment.

But Thomas, while keeping the departures of Mill from
Stephanus, adds a number of other departures; such as the
following: Matt. 23 : 13, 14, reversing the order of the two
verses; Mark 8 : 24, omitting ὅτι and ὁρῶ; Luke 1 : 35, adding ἐκ σου; Luke 15 : 26, omitting αὐτοῦ; John 18 : 20, reading πάντοθεν οἱ for πάντοτε οἱ; Acts 7 : 44, inserting ἐν before
τῇ ἐρήμῳ; Acts 9 : 35, Σάρωνα for Σαρωνᾶν; Acts 17 : 25,
καὶ τὰ πάντα for κατὰ πάντα; Acts 21 : 3, ἀναφανέντες for
ἀναφάναντες; Acts 21 : 8, ἤλθομεν [sic] for ἤλθον; Acts 24 :
13, omitting με; Rom. 7 : 6, ἀποθανόντος for ἀποθανόντες;
Rom. 8 : 11, διὰ τοῦ ἐνοικοῦντος . . . πνεύματος [sic] for διὰ
τὸ ἐνοικοῦν . . . πνεῦμα; Rom. 12 : 11, Κυρίῳ for καιρῷ; 1
Cor. 15 : 31, ὑμετέραν for ἡμετέραν; 2 Cor. 7 : 12, ἡμῶν τὴν
ὑπὲρ ὑμῶν for ὑμῶν τὴν ὑπὲρ ἡμῶν; 1 Tim. 1 : 4, οἰκοδομίαν
for οἰκονομίαν; Rev. 5 : 11, adding καὶ ἦν ὁ ἀριθμὸς αὐτῶν
μυριάδες μυριάδων; Rev. 11 : 1, adding καὶ ὁ ἄγγελος εἱστήκει;
Rev. 11 : 2, ἔξωθεν for ἔσωθεν. These specimens show
nothing but editorial judgment, together with a Beza or a
late Elzevir text, or both, from which to select the variant
readings. It is not necessary to pass upon the editorial
judgment here displayed—which is sometimes good and

1633, and at least the Leyden 24mo of 1641) of τοῦ νόμου in Romans 7 : 2.
The edition of 1678 corrects also the error, existing in *all* the preceding editions, of ναῷ for λαῷ, in Revelation 3 : 12. This last, very widespread, error
of the Stephanic-Elzevir family of texts appears to have been first committed in
the R. Stephanus edition of 1551.

sometimes bad. The facts we are concerned with here are, first, that the work of an editor is manifest, and that better than might have been expected from the Latin of the title-page; and second, that the profession in the title that the text is an accurate reprint of Mill is intentionally false. But the title was copied from English editions which had made the same false pretense—already for nearly a century. And not only so, but the lauded *textus receptus* has been perpetually juggled with in the same way; so that it is rare to find two editions that agree exactly, or one that bears out the professions of its titlepage. The horror with which the simple-minded venerators of the *textus receptus* shrink from the latest critical texts and the latest revised translations is a mild sensation in comparison with the confusion which a little closer examination of its various *exemplaria* would bring upon them. The *textus receptus* of to-day—or of former times, for that matter—is nothing but a shadow and a ghost, which its professed adherents and admirers would generally be the last to recognize as an acquaintance. The critical student finds no limit to his astonishment at the bigoted ignorance, and the unquestioning adherence to the grossest errors, which pervade the English and American works in this respect from the early portion of the last century nearly to the present day. If the zealous defenders of tradition had but investigated only a few of the more prominent matters, instead of blindly following the lead of the (generally virulent) opponents of desirable reform, it would have been better for Christianity and the truth.

Following the order of genealogy, instead of the order of time, we come upon a second edition, virtually, of this Greek Testament of Thomas; published at Boston, in 1814. Its title proper differs slightly from that of the other in the lines, but not in the words. Instead of the caduceus with the cornucopias, the ornament here is two reclining figures supporting the open Bible, with the verse 1 Cor. 15 : 22, in Greek, underneath for a motto. Then the words " BOSTONIÆ : | Ex-cudebat ESAIAS THOMAS, JUN. | Typis WATSON &

BANGS. | 1814." Its form is 12mo, pp. 478, like the other. The accessory matter is the same chronological table, but differently arranged, and without signature. The Latin for " Isaiah " is this time spelled after the ordinary fashion, " Esaias," on the titlepage.[1] Otherwise this edition so nearly resembles the last that a very close look is needed to see the difference. It coincides with the former, page for page and line for line, and almost letter for letter, only it spells out most of the ligatures and employs more recent forms of type for some of the letters. A mutilated copy of this edition might also be recognized by its omission of the chapter-number as a running title at the top of the pages, and by the erroneous page-number 231, in place of 431. It agrees with the former in all the departures from Mill, above-mentioned, and adds a few more of its own besides. Of these last are: Matt. 6 : 6, the Erasmian ταμεῖον for Mill's ταμιεῖον (a variation of which the more recent editions of Pritius, or the title of Schmidt's Greek N. T. Concordance, may have been a nearer source); Mark 6 : 33, προσῆλθον for προῆλθον (perhaps an error, but committed in the earlier Brylinger series of editions, from 1542 onward); 1 Cor. 15 : 33, the ancient χρῆστὰ [thus accented] restored in place of the metrically adapted χρῆσθ᾽ [*sic*]; and 2 John 1, ἐκλεκτῇ for Ἐκλεκτῇ. It is, however, a very tolerable Mill.

Following still the order of genealogy—almost every one is familiar with Bagster's " Polymicrian Greek Testament," provided with its (Greenfield's) Lexicon, and other conveniences for the beginner. It first appeared in England in 1829. Of

---

[1] Concerning the variation in the Latin form of this name, I subjoin a note communicated to me by Dr. F. J. A. Hort. Speaking of the spelling adopted by Thomas in the first edition, he says : " He merely followed the spelling of the official editions of the Vulgate, and much modern usage. Nor is it certain that Jerome never used Is., as better representing the Hebrew. In his etymology of proper names in the Acts (*Onomastica*, p. 69 Lagarde) he says 'Esaias salus Domini : verum apud Hebræos ab I littera sumit exordium;' and while he places the name under E in three books, he places it under I in Matthew. I observe, too, that the Codex Amiatinus is said to have *Esaiæ* in Isaiah i. 1, and *Isaias* in ii. 1." We have, of course, abundant authority of *usage*, at least, for the stricter form Iesaias or Jesaias.

the readings which Reuss uses in his *Bibliotheca* as a means of classifying Greek Testaments in families, this edition seems to vary from Mill's text in only three: viz. Acts 17 : 25, καὶ πάντα for κατὰ πάντα; Acts 21 : 3, ἀναφανέντες for ἀναφάναντες; and Colossians 1 : 2, Κολοσσαῖς for Κολασσαῖς; all intended to be adoptions of Beza or Elzevir readings, only the first is a misprint for καὶ τὰ πάντα. This English edition has been repeated many times without date; and of the copies imported to America, some bear the imprint of Wiley, New York; and some others that of Lippincott, Philadelphia.

But an actual reprint has appeared in America,[1] issued many times, both with and without date, and with different imprints. Its title and form are as follows: "Η ΚΑΙΝΗ ΔΙΑΘΗΚΗ. | NOVUM TESTAMENTUM | AD | EXEMPLAR MILLIANUM, | cum | emendationibus et lectionibus Griesbachii, | præcipuis vocibus ellipticis, | thematibus omnium vocum difficiliorum, | atque locis Scripturæ parallelis. | Studio et labore | Gulielmi Greenfield. | Hanc editionem primam Americanam, | summâ curâ recensuit, atque mendis quàm plurimis expurgavit, | JOSEPHUS P. ENGLES, A. M." 32mo, pp. 571; lexicon, pp. iv. 281.

As the title states, it was edited by Joseph P. Engles, A. M.,[2]

---

[1] Reuss (*Bibliotheca N. T. Gr.*, p. 154) confounds this edition with a New Testament published by Joshua Leavitt, at New York, in 1832, and again by A. S. Barnes & Co., New York, 1846; and I followed the same error in my previous publication. But I have ascertained that that New Testament is only an *English* New Testament, with " Η ΚΑΙΝΗ ΔΙΑΘΗΚΗ " at the top of the title-page, besides a *Greek* title (in addition to the English one) for every separate book of the N. T. The book is described in O'Callaghan's American Bibles, pp. 219, 294. O'Callaghan is quite correct, but it is easy to obtain an erroneous impression both from his description and from his index. The book is a reprint of the English Polymicrian, and was first made by Joshua Leavitt. The plates were afterwards sold at auction, and bought by A. S. Barnes, who issued the edition of 1846. He sold them again in 1862 or '63, when they were bought by Warren F. Draper of Andover, who issued a third edition, in 1863. A little more care on the part of Reuss or myself would have detected the error; for its pages are 546, and its stereotyper was James Conner of New York. The stereotypers of the Engles Gr. N. T. were L. Johnson & Co. of Philadelphia.

[2] Joseph Patterson Engles (b. Jan. 3., 1793, d. April 14, 1861) was a Philadelphian, graduated at the University of Pennsylvania in 1811; in 1813 co-master of the grammar-school of that institution; 1817–45 master of the Clas-

whose claim to have purged it of many errors committed in the original edition is by no means unfounded. Besides the correction of errors, and several minor changes in the text, it chiefly differs from the English edition in the substitution of an English preface for the Latin one of the London editions. In this English preface an apparent error of the Latin is made more definitely an error by stating that the text "is that commonly called the received text, which was first published at Leyden, A, D. 1624, by Elzevir, and republished in folio at Oxford, by Mill, A. D. 1707." Which shows that the editor's knowledge on that point was at best but second-hand. As to text, he retains the three above-mentioned instances of departure from the Millio-Stephanic to the Beza-Elzevir, correcting, however, the error of the London edition in Acts 17 : 25, and reading καὶ τὰ πάντα.[1] All the perfect copies of this edition seem to contain the familiar plate with the words

sical Institute of which he was one of the founders; 1845 publishing agent of the Presbyterian Board of Publication. He was the author of several books, mostly for the young. He was a college classmate of that Christian poet and philanthropist the late Rev. Dr. William Augustus Muhlenberg, who often said, and has left the statement in print, that for what he was in life and work, he owed more to Joseph P. Engles than to any other man.

[1] In making his corrections, the author made use of "a very accurate copy of Mill's Testament, published at Oxford in 1825; the various readings, with Griesbach's Testament, published in Cambridge, New England, in 1809." This Oxford edition of 1825 is not very easy to find, and is not noticed in Reuss's *Bibliotheca.* If it was one of the series which reproduces the Oxford ed. of 1805 (which is rather a Bowyer text than a Mill), Engles could not have followed it; and he certainly does not agree with the common beautiful Oxford 16mo which professes to follow the Oxford copy of 1825. In order to show how Engles differs from the professed reprints of Mill, and how these reprints differ one from another, as well as the relation of these differences to certain important or standard texts, the following collation of specimen places is appended. In the table, Bagst. is the Bagster Polymicrian; M, the original Mill of 1707; K, Küster's Mill; O₅, the Oxford reprint of Mill, of 1805; O₂₅, the common Oxford 16mo, which professes to follow the edition of 1825; Th (alone), Thomas of 1800 and 1814 (when they differ the date is annexed to show the reading of each); Bez (alone), Beza's folios of 1565 and 1598, and 8vo edd. of 1567, 1580, and 1604 (the date is annexed when they differ); Elz (alone), the Elzevirs of 1624 and 1633 (the date is given when they differ); HS, Henry Stephens of 1587; P, Pickering of 1828; G, the American Griesbach of 1809; WH, Wescott and Hort; T, Von Gebhardt's Tischendorf of 1881 :

for " The New Testament " in forty-eight different languages;
though the London editions sometimes omit it.

Luke 6 : 9. ὑμᾶς τι· *Engles*, Bagst. M. K. O₅. Th. P. Elz.
ὑμᾶς, τί O₂₅. Bez (Bez '67. ὑμᾶς τι,). HS.; ὑμᾶς· Τί G.
ὑμᾶς, εἰ WH.; ὑμᾶς εἰ T.

Luke 7 : 12. καὶ αὕτη χήρα *Engles*, O₂₅. P. Elz. G.
καὶ αὐτῇ χήρᾳ Bagst. M. O₅. Bez. HS.
καὶ αὕτη ἦν χήρα K. Th. T. WH (αὕτη).

Luke 15 : 26. *omit.* αὐτοῦ *post* παίδων *Engles*, Th. P. Bez. Elz. HS. G. WH. T.
add. αὐτοῦ Bagst. M. K. O₅. O₂₅.

Luke 19 : 4. συκομορέαν *Engles*, Th. P. Bez '67. Elz '24. G. WH. T.
συκομωραίαν Bagst. M. K. O₅. O₂₅. Elz '33. Bez '65. '98. '80.
1604. HS.

Luke 20 : 31. ἑπτὰ, καὶ οὐ *Engles*, Bagst. M. O₅. Bez '80. 1604.
ἑπτὰ οὐ K. Bez '65. '98. WH. T.; ἑπτά· οὐ G.
ἑπτά· καὶ οὐ Th. O₂₅. P. Elz. Bez '67. HS.

John 6 : 28. ποιῶμεν *Engles*, P. Bez '65. '67. '98. '80. Elz. HS. G. WH. T.
ποιοῦμεν Bagst. M. K. Th. O₅. O₂₅. Bez. 1604.

John 13 : 30. νύξ. (31.)ʼΟτε οὖν ἐξῆλθε *Engles*, P. Bez (Bez '67. νύξ·). Elz. HS.
G. WH. T.
νὺξ ὅτε οὖν ἐξῆλθε Bagst. M. Th. K. O₅. O₂₅.

John 19 : 12. ἑαυτὸν *Engles*, G. WH. T.
αὐτὸν Bagst. M. K. Th. O₅. O₂₅. P. Bez '65. '67. '98. '80. Elz. HS.
αὐτὸν Bez 1604.

Acts 5 : 18. αὐτῶν *Engles*, O₂₅.
αὐτῶν Bagst. M. K. Th. O₅. O₂₅. P. Bez. Elz. HS. G.
omit. WH. T.

Acts 7 : 44. ἐν τῇ ἐρήμῳ *Engles*, Bagst. K. Th. O₅. O₂₅. P. Bez. Elz. HS. G.
WH. T.
τῇ ἐρήμῳ (*omit.* ἐν) M.

Acts 21 : 8. ἤλθομεν *Engles*, Th. P. Bez '67. '80. 1604. Elz. HS. G. T.; ἤλ-
θαμεν WH.
ἤλθον Bagst. M. K. O₅. O₂₅. Bez '65. '98.

Acts 24 : 13. *omit.* με *Engles*, Th. P. Bez. Elz. HS. G. WH. T.
add. με *ante* δύνανται Bagst. M. K. O₅. O₂₅.

Acts 26 : 20. ἀπήγγελλον *Engles*, P. Bez '67. '80. 1604. Elz. HS. G. WH. T.
ἀπαγγέλλων Bagst. M. K. Th. O₅. O₂₅. Bez '65. '98.

Acts 27 : 13. ἆσσον *Engles*, P. O₂₅. Bez. Elz '24. HS. G. WH. T.
ʼΑσσον Bagst. M. K. Th. O₅. Elz '33.

Acts 27 : 17. Σύρτιν *Engles*, Bagst. Th. O₅. P. Bez. Elz. HS. G. WH. T.
σύρτιν M. K. O₂₅.

2 Cor. 7 : 12. ἡμῶν τὴν ὑπὲρ ὑμῶν *Engles*, Th. P. Bez. Elz. G.
ὑμῶν τὴν ὑπὲρ ἡμῶν Bagst. M. K. O₅. O₂₅. WH. T.
ὑμῶν τὴν ὑπὲρ ὑμῶν HS.

Coloss. 1 : 2. Κολοσσαῖς *Engles*, Bagst. Th. O₅. P. Bez. Elz. G. WH. T.
Κολασσαῖς M. K. O₂₅. HS.

This edition was prepared by Mr. Engles for the publisher, Henry Perkins, of Philadelphia, who has kept possession of the plates ever since, printing for himself and other publishers according to the demand. It first appeared in February, 1838, at Philadelphia, with the imprint "Philadelphiæ: Sumptibus Henrici Perkins. Bostoniæ: Perkins et Marvin." The lexicon (Greenfield's, with Engles's revision) followed in September, 1839. Otherwise, except a few early copies bound separately for convenience, the New Testament and Lexicon have always been issued together in one volume. Other issues are as follows: Philadelphia, H. Perkins, 1839, 1840, 1841, 1846, 1848, 1850; Philadelphia, Perkins and Purves, 1844, 1846; Philadelphia, Clark and Hesser, 1853, 1854; Philadelphia, H. C. Peck and Theodore Bliss, 1854, 1855, 1856; also without date, Philadelphia, H. C. Peck and Theo. Bliss, or sometimes simply Peck and Bliss (several issues in 1854, 1855, and 1856); Philadelphia, Theodore Bliss, & Co. (from 1856, the year of Mr. Peck's death, onward); and Philadelphia, Lippincott. There were many repetitions of the undated issues, but their exact number cannot now be ascertained. Until 1840, the names of Perkins and Marvin were given as the Boston publishers; but in 1841 their names were replaced by those of Ives and Dennet; after which no Boston publisher's name appears in the imprint. Benjamin Perkins, of the firm of Perkins and Marvin, was a brother of the Philadelphia Henry Perkins. All the copies of this edition hitherto mentioned have "Hanc editionem primam Americanam" on the title-page; the plates having never been changed except as to date and imprint. It has always been a favorite edition among students, and as a pocket companion. It is becoming rather hard to pick up in the antiquarian bookstores.

1 Thess. 2 : 15. ἡμᾶς *Engles*, O₅. P. Bez. Elz. HS. G. WH. T.
ὑμᾶς Bagst. M. K. Th. O₂₅.

2 John 1. ἐκλεκτῇ *Engles*, Bagst. Th 1814. P. O₅. O₂₅. Bez. Elz. HS. G. WH. T.
Ἐκλεκτῇ M. K. Th 1800.

2 John 13. ἐκλεκτῆς *Engles*, Bagst. P. O₅. O₂₅. Bez '65. '98. 1604. Elz. HS. G. WH. T.
Ἐκλεκτῆς M. K. Th. Bez '80.

2

A second edition of this New Testament, with the plates carefully corrected, was issued by Henry Perkins, in 1883, at Philadelphia, with the following title: " H ΚΑΙΝΗ ΔΙΑΘΗΚΗ | Novum Testamentum | Græce | cum | emendationibus et lectionibus Griesbachii | præcipuis vocibus ellipticis | thematibus omnium vocum difficiliorum | atque locis Scripturæ parallelis | e recognitione | Gulielmi Greenfield | recensum atque mendis expurgatum cura | Josephi P Engles A M | emendatius edidit adnotationemque criticam addidit | Isaacus H Hall A M LL B Ph D." (pp. 631.) The additional matter contained in this edition is a Preface to the Second Edition, and a Supplement, containing the " Various Readings adopted by the English and American Revisers, 1881," with other matter explanatory and critical. The Supplement includes the readings preferred (in text and margin) in the Appendix to the Revised Version of the English New Testament. The " Various Readings " are kept within the bounds of the editions of Scrivener and Palmer, published at Oxford and Cambridge, respectively, in 1881 ; except that a few misprints of these editions are corrected, and the few changes required by the preferences of the American Committee are drawn from another source.

Another of the Mill family is that of the Rev. J. A. Spencer,[1] under the following title: *"H KAINH ΔΙΑΘΗΚΗ* | The | Four Gospels and Acts of the Apostles | in Greek. | With English Notes, Critical, Philological, and Exe- | getical ; Maps, Indexes, etc. | Together with the Epistles and Apocalypse. | The whole forming the complete text of | The New Testament. | For the use of Schools, Colleges, and Theological Seminaries. | By Rev. J. A. Spencer, A. M., | author of | ' The Christian Instructed,' ' History of the English Reformation,' etc. | τὸ καλὸν κἀγαθόν. | New York: | Harper and Brothers, Publishers, 82 Cliff Street. | 1847." 12mo, pp. xii., 611. This title is fairly descriptive, except as to the author himself. It was evidently intended first as a class-book, and

<hr />

[1] Jesse Ames Spencer, D. D., b. 1816. For a sketch of his life and numerous works, see *Johnson's Cyclopædia*, iv. p. 426.

to contain only the Gospels and Acts—which indeed were issued separately the same year, 1847, and again in 1859. Other editions of the entire book were issued by the same publishers in 1852, 1859, 1860, 1865, 1868, 1875, and 1877. Only the Gospels and Acts have notes; but the Epistles and Revelation have a little accessory matter in the shape of general introductions and tables. Its text is very nearly that of Burton (Oxford, England, 1831, and several subsequent editions), which departed from Mill to Elzevir in fourteen noticeable places, which may be found enumerated in Prof. Dr. Eduard Reuss's *Bibliotheca Novi Testamenti Græci* (Brunsvigæ, 1872), p. 154. Spencer professes to adopt Burton's text, and to venture to differ therewith only on a few occasions, and then principally in the pointing, the use of capital letters, and other particulars of a like grade of importance. But he leaves Mill for Elzevir in two places more than Burton, viz., in the last two of the three just mentioned of the Polymicrian.

One more edition, and that a noteworthy one, exhibits Mill's text professedly; or, to speak more accurately, it professes to follow " Bagster's edition [1851] of Mill's reprint of Stephens's third edition (1550)." This is the elaborate Greek-English work of the American Bible Union, in 4to, intended as provisional and preliminary to their proposed new English translation of the Bible. This work was published in parts, but, so far as I can learn, was never completed, so as to include the whole of the New Testament. As to text, I cannot speak from personal examination as to its variations, either from the original Mill or from the Bagster edition which it took as a standard. In the small portion I have examined it leaves the Mill text for the Elzevir in a few places; for example, that already noticed by Reuss (*Bibliotheca*, p. 157), Rev. 3 : 1, inserting ἑπτὰ before πνεύματα. But to have changed the *text* materially would have been a measure too bold for the contemplated purpose of the work, and for the times as well. The notes of this edition, and the introductions to some portions, give it a thoroughly critical character; and as such it should be classed.

The portions that have appeared, so far as I can learn, are the following; all published at New York by the American Bible Union, but bearing also the imprint, Louisville, Bible Revision Association, and London, Trübner & Co.:

1854. 2 Peter, 1, 2, and 3 John, Judas, and Revelation, pp. xi., 253; anonymous, but by John Lillie.

1855. Matthew, Chapters I., II., and III., pp. 52; anonymous, but by Orrin B. Judd. The same, reissued in 1858, is called "second edition."

1856. John, pp. xvi., 171; anonymous, but by a Mr. Morton. Also the same, reissued in 1859, and again in 1864.

1856. 1 and 2 Thessalonians, pp. viii., 73; anonymous, but by John Lillie. The titlepage states that it was by the same person as the editor of 2 Peter, 1, 2, and 3 John, Judas, and Revelation. (Also, London, England, 1858.)

1857. Ephesians, pp. vi., 39; anonymous, but by N. N. Whiting. Also, the same reissued in 1864.

1857. Hebrews, pp. vi., 90; anonymous, but shown by the prefatory matter to have been done by the editor of Ephesians, or N. N. Whiting.

1858. Acts, pp. iv., 224; anonymous, but by Alexander Campbell.

1858. Mark, pp. vi., 134; anonymous, but by N. N. Whiting. Also, the same reissued in 1866.

1860. Matthew, pp. xxx., 171; T. J. Conant. Also, the same reissued in 1866.

1860. Luke, pp. viii., 273; anonymous, but by N. N. Whiting. Also, the same reissued in 1866.

1860. 1 and 2 Timothy and Titus, pp. vi., 78; anonymous, but the prefatory matter shows that they were done by the editor of Ephesians, Hebrews, Mark, and Luke; or, N. N. Whiting.

1860. Philemon, pp. 44; anonymous, but by H. B. Hackett. The preface is dated "Newton Centre, April 13, 1860." This last was issued again the same year, in small 4to, or 18mo, pp. 90. Unlike the others, this part omits the Common English Version. It is rather a general commentary than strictly like the rest of the series.

1861. The various parts, each bearing its own date (together with the published parts of the Old Testament), bound in one immense volume, with a new title, "The Sacred Scriptures," etc.

Although the American Bible Union and its work were a Baptist enterprise, John Lillie, the author of several of the above preliminary revisions, was a Presbyterian clergyman. In critical and scholarly character there is a wide difference between the several parts; the Matthew by Dr. Conant, the Philemon by Dr. Hackett, and the several parts by Dr. John Lillie, being of a much higher grade than the rest. The volume which comprises the Gospel of John, indeed, was published against the protest of certain prominent men of the Baptist denomination (of whom one was the late Dr. Hackett), who considered it "discreditable to the scholarship of the American Bible Union." And, in the language of a modern (Baptist) critic, its "pages swarm with blunders."

It is a common error that these preliminary or provisional publications were the joint work of a number of men. That may be true with regard to some parts of their *English version*, but it is not so with regard to the Greek text and its immediate accessories. In each case it was the work of one author. Other provisional work for some of the remaining books was done in manuscript, as the Epistle to the Galatians by Dr. Philip Schaff (who is German Reformed as to denomination); and the first Epistle of Peter and the Epistle of James by John Lillie, but they were never printed.

III. THE LEUSDEN (ELZEVIR) EDITIONS.

THE next family to appear in America was that of the Leusden editions. The first example was the Greek-Latin New Testament published by Bradford, at Philadelphia, in 1806. The titlepage is preceded by a short false title (consisting of the first six lines of the true), and reads as follows: "*H KAINH | ΔIAΘHKH.* | Novum | TESTAMENTUM, | cum versione Latina | Ariæ Montani, | in quo tum selecti versiculi 1900, quibus omnes Novi | Testamenti voces continentur, asteriscis | notantur; | tum omnes & singulæ voces, semel vel sæpius occurrentes, | peculiari nota distinguuntur. | Auctore | Johanne Leusden, Professore. | Editio Prima Amer icana: | qua plurima Londiniensis errata, diligentissime ani- | mad- | versa, corriguntur: | Cura Johannis Watts. | Philadel- phiæ: | Ex Officina Classica: | Impensis S. F. Bradford. | 1806." The book is a 12mo, pp. 561, pretty accurately printed, and altogether a credit to the publishers and to the times.

As already seen, this can be the "editio prima *Americana*" only as a Leusden edition; for it is the second of the Greek Testament absolutely. The corrector named on the titlepage was the printer, as we see from the note at the end of the book: "Excudebat J. Watts." In this edition an editor's work has little or no place. As it professes, it is a reprint of the famous edition of John Leusden, in which 1900 select verses are marked with a *, as containing together all the words of the New Testament; and words which occur only once, or very rarely, are marked by a † and ‡ respectively. For its immediate original, the "London edition" mentioned on the titlepage, we have three from which to choose. One of these was issued at Leyden by the Wetsteins in 1772, but

22

it bears also on the titlepage the imprint "Londini, apud Joannem Nourse." The second so closely resembles this one, line for line and page for page, that it requires close scrutiny to see that they actually are different issues. It was published at London in 1794, and bears the imprint of six different publishing houses, of which the first named is F. Wingrave. The third, dated 1804, is of exactly the same description as the second, except that it contains some misprints not found in the other two, and has the imprint of *seven* different publishing houses, of which the first named is F. Wingrave. The form of each is 12mo, pp. 699, on sheets a trifle smaller than the American Bradford. Those of 1772 and 1794 have the well known Wetstein maps, which are lacking in the edition of 1804, as well as in the American editions.

The text of this edition need not be dwelt upon at length, since, except in just one noticeable change, it is pretty purely the Elzevir of 1678. The first Leusden appeared at Utrecht in 1675,[1] with nearly the Elzevir text of 1670; but the second

---

[1] As this Leusden of 1675 has greatly puzzled the bibliographers (see, for example, Masch's Le Long's *Bibliotheca Sacra*, Pars I. Cap. II. Sect. I. ¿ XCVII.; Baumgarten's *Nachrichten von Merkwürdigern Büchern*, Bd. IV., pp. 383, 384; Goeze's *Verzeichniss*, I. 57; Adler's *Bibliotheca Biblica*, etc., *Lorckiana*, p. 99), it is as well to say that Reuss is undoubtedly right in his description of the two books (*Bibliotheca N. T. Gr.*, pp. 122, 123, 131), whose confusion has made the trouble and aroused the suspicion. The book which Masch, Baumgarten, Goeze, and Adler describe, with more or less perplexity and suspicion, as the first Leusden, has indeed the same title as the genuine Leusden of 1675, the same date, and the same place and publisher, besides being printed with the same font of type. The title of the genuine edition reads: " Ἡ' ΚΑΙΝΠ᾽ | ΔΙΑΘΗ΄ΚΗ. | Novum | TESTAMENTUM | *Cum* | Distinctione versiculorum | *Qui omnes* | Novi Testamenti voces continent. | [Ornament, an armillary sphere.] | ULTRA-JECTI, | Ex Officinâ Antonii Smytegelt. | cIɔ Iɔ Lxxv." The title to the other book, as I learn from Adler's description, has for ornament, in place of the sphere, " facies angeli aliquot floribus cincta." (I have copies of both books, but the latter lacks the titlepage.) The genuine, in accordance with the statement of the titlepage, has the [1900] verses marked with a * as containing together all the words of the New Testament (the † and ‡ for their several purposes were not added till 1688), but no trace of them exists in the other. The genuine contains two prefatory pages ("Johannes Leusden Lectori benevoli S. P."), explaining, among other things, his plan about the 1900 verses, which were selected, under his direction, by the " Ornatissimus Juvenis D. Adamus ab Halen, Rotterædamo-Batavus " (nothing is said about this Adam van Halen in the later prefaces), and dated Kal. Nov. 1674. It also has the common table of quota-

Leusden, 1688, struck out a new path, following the Elzevir of 1678. A series of editions kept this latter text till 1740, when the change above referred to was introduced: viz., the adding καὶ στραφεὶς πρὸς τοὺς μαθητὰς, εἶπε at the beginning of Luke 10 : 22. It was this edition of 1740, or rather its Greek-Latin form of 1741, from which descended, by mere reproduction, the editions of 1772, 1794, and 1804 above mentioned; either of which, again, may have been the immediate parent of the American Bradford. Of this ancestral series, the first edition was published at Amsterdam and London; at Amsterdam by the two houses of Boom and Van Soemeren, and in London by Sam. Smith. The other editions of the series were all issued by the Wetsteins at Amsterdam. A double group of offshoots of this Leusden edition, each with its very trifling variations, appeared during the same period. One of the two started at Frankfurt a. M., 1692, edited by Rudolph Leusden, son of John. The other, more nearly conformed to the Elzevir of 1633, was published at Leyden from 1699 onward. It is of a form rather minute, and probably the first Greek Testament ever stereotyped. It usually bears the imprint of Luchtmans. Then followed a long series of branches, more or less different from Leusden's original and from each other, issued by various publishers at various places in Germany.

In the same year with the Bradford edition just mentioned, the same publisher issued the same Greek text without the Latin, calling it "Editio Secunda Americana;" but it is second only as a Leusden. Watts is named as the corrector and printer of this edition also. It is a 12mo, like the last, pp. 286.

tions from the Old Testament made in the New. But the other edition has no prefatory matter, nor similar table; and its text is different, being a reprint of that of the edition of Fell (Anonymous, Oxonii, e Theatro Sheldoniano, 1675). The genuine is a 16mo (we should now say a 32mo), numbered pages 703 (really, pp. xvi. 704), and is printed with lines running the whole width of the page. The other is a 24mo, pp. 611, though a thicker book, and is printed with two columns to the page. The publisher's use of the Leusden title for this latter edition is no more than has been done in America during the present century, as will be seen farther on, p. 37.

The next edition of Leusden's New Testament appeared at New York in 1821; the title being like the Bradford edition as far as applicable; the note of publication being " Novi-Eboraci: Typis et Impensis Geòrgii Long, No. 71, Pearl Street. 1821." This is a 12mo of small sized sheets, pp. 699; being page for page, line for line, and word for word, a close copy of the editions of 1772, 1794, and 1804 above referred to; but in every respect save thickness it is a smaller book. It might be called a "facsimile" of either; only, as it copies the misprints of the edition of 1804, the last is doubtless its immediate parent. (One of these misprints, for example, is in John 19 : 30 Τετέλησται for Τετέλεσται.)

These three editions, the two Bradfords and the Long, are the only Leusden editions, so far as I know, ever published in America; though one phenomenon of the book-stores and libraries, to be mentioned farther on, speaks otherwise to the unwary.

In this connection is to be mentioned an edition of Macknight's Epistles, which appeared under the following title: "A New | Literal Translation | from the Original Greek, | of all the | Apostolical Epistles. | With | A Commentary, and Notes, | Philological, Critical, Explanatory, and Practical. | To which is added, | a History of the Apostle Paul. | By James Macknight, D. D. | Author of a Harmony of the Gospels, &c. | In Six Volumes. | To which is prefixed | an Account of the Life of the Author. | . . . | Boston : | Published by W. Wells and T. B. Wait & Co. | T. B. Wait & Co. Printers | 1810." It is an 8vo; vol. i. pp. xiv. 503 (Romans); vol. ii. pp. [iv.] 471 (1 and 2 Corinthians); vol. iii. pp. [iv.] 561 (Galatians to Colossians); vol. iv. pp. [iv.] 409 (Thessalonians to Philemon); vol. v. pp. [iv.] 571 (James to 2 Peter); vol. vi. pp. [iv.] 433 (John to Jude). It is printed with breathings, but without accents. The General Preface and the preliminary Essays contain a great deal of useful matter, and the foot-notes show much critical study on particular points, though no thoroughness or ripeness as a general critic. A foot-note on pages 36–39 gives a very fair historical account of the principal Greek

New Testaments, from the Complutensian down to Bengel, though strangely mixed with error. For instance, he speaks of an Elzevir Gr. N. T. of 1622, and another "two years after this . . . corrected, as Beza [d. 1605!] informs us, by not a few persons, eminent for learning and piety."

"The text of the Greek New Testament followed in this translation," as we are informed in the General Preface, vol. i. p. 35, "is the one in common use;" which the author followed because he conceived it to have been "settled according to the opinion of learned men in different countries, who compared a great number of MSS, and fixed on the readings which appeared to them best supported." But "the author hath altered the accenting [accents are wanting in this American edition] and pointing of the common edition in a few instances, in order to obtain a better and more perspicuous sense of the passages." But the readings of Mill's "noble edition " "are by no means to be admitted," for reasons which the author found in Whitby's *Examen*. What particular edition "in common use" was followed by the author, is not so certain. He himself believed it to be that of R. Stephens of 1550 (see vol. i., pp. 38, 39, foot-note). But an examination shows that it is much nearer the Elzevir of 1678. It appears to agree with the latter against Stephens in every case where the two differ, except only in 2 Timothy 4 : 13 (reading φαιλόνην) and 1 Peter 2 : 21 (reading ἡμῶν, ἡμῖν).

Further to be mentioned in this connection, as presenting a text of the same general family, is the peculiarly constructed Harmony of the Gospels by the Rev. Dr. James Strong. Its text is nearly the Elzevir of 1633. This is a 12mo, pp. iv. 624, published at New York by the Harpers in 1854; also, the same year, by J. C. Riker, and again by the Harpers in 1859.

It may be added that these five books are the only American representatives of the European *textus receptus;* and that not one of them is a perfect representative of either of the patterns—that is, of either the Elzevir of 1624 or that of 1633. They are apparently nearer the Elzevir of 1678, but certainly not identical with it.

IV. THE GRIESBACH EDITIONS.

The next family to appear came in order of time next to the Bradford Leusdens of 1806; starting with the most important of our early issues. This was the reprint of Griesbach's Manual (Leipzig, Goeschen, 1805), his third edition and most finished text; issued at Cambridge, at the University Press, in 1809. The form of this reprint is 8vo, pp. xxiv. 615. Its titlepage differs from that of its original by adding the words: "Cantabrigiæ Nov-Anglorum 1809. Typis Academicis; sumtibus [*sic*] W. Wells et W. Hilliard." The editor is understood to have been W. Wells, who was a scholar, as well as one of the publishers. It has a title-page for each volume (the second volume beginning with Acts), but the paging is continuous throughout, disregarding in the enumeration, however, the titlepage to volume ii., and the blank pages on each side of it. The whole is a pretty accurate piece of work; and adds to the original only one page of matter: the publishers' dedication to the President and Fellows of Harvard University. This edition had a deservedly wide circulation; and it has been taken as the basis of all the Griesbach texts published in this country—though its successors have generally followed it only *longo intervallo*. This edition was used by Mr. Engles, as he states in his English preface to the American Polymicrian Greek Testament noticed above, in verifying the Griesbach readings given in that volume.

At the time of its publication, this book is said to have been hailed by one party with joy—" with an *Io triumphe*," as one of the old-school Biblical scholars informs me—as a denominational weapon, and the annihilator of their opponents; while by the latter it was looked upon with timidity, not only as the destroyer of proof-texts and the discloser of the sandy foundation of innumerable sermons, but as a would-be unsettler of the foundation of the New Testament itself. But the telegraph did not exist in those days, and those hopes and fears and antagonisms remained local and temporary. It was impossible to make a critical edition of the New Testament a badge of orthodoxy or heresy on either side; and the book came speedily into use and preference among the more enlightened clergymen of that generation, in all denominations. Andover Theological Seminary appears to have taken the lead in this favorable movement, among representatives of the timid side. At all events, a Harmony of the Gospels with this text was soon prepared for use in that institution. From that day onward, America has not ceased to possess critical texts of native print, although she cannot say, like Germany, that her scholars have issued no Elzevir text since 1775.[1] The publication of this Griesbach in America was no common event.

The Gospels of this text, accompanied by a vocabulary, were issued at Boston in 1825, by " Cummings, Hilliard, and Company—Washington Street." The type is the same as that used in the volume just mentioned; the form 8vo, pp. iii. 240; Lexicon, pp. 71. The marginal readings are omitted. This volume was " prepared in consequence of the new arrangement of the studies in Greek, preparatory to admission into the University at Cambridge," " the Corporation having

---

[1] This is true of German scholars and publishers as such. The British and Foreign Bible Society, from at least 1856 to the present year, has published various Mill-Elzevir texts at Cologne and elsewhere in Germany, to the strong distaste, if not the scandal, of the German scholars. Says Reuss of the British Cologne edition of 1856 : " Pretio vili studiosis nostris venditur in ipsa Germania excusus liber, scilicet ut criticæ editiones puriorem textum representantes eorum oculis facilius subducantur." And Von Gebhardt's Greek-German New Testament is sold at a low price with the (politely) avowed intention of opposition to those texts of the British Society. Since the publication of the Revised Version of the English New Testament, and the issue by the British Society of its circular to translators, allowing them to conform their work to the text of that Version, the Society may feel more at liberty to circulate a corrected original along with its corrected versions.

substituted Jacobs' Greek Reader and the Four Gospels for the Collectanea Græca Minora and the whole of the New Testament." The titlepage, also, says that it is "Designed for the use of schools." The (anonymous) editor of the text was N. L. Frothingham.

As already indicated, this text next appeared in Moses Stuart's edition of Newcome's Harmony of the Gospels, under the following title: "A | Harmony in Greek | of the | Gospels, | with | Notes, | by William Newcome, D. D., | Dublin, 1788: | reprinted from the | text and select various readings | of | Griesbach, | by the Junior Class in the | Theological Seminary | at Andover, under the superintendence of Moses Stuart, | associate professor of sacred literature in said | seminary. | Andover: | Printed by Flagg and Gould. | 1814." This appears to be the first Greek Harmony of the Gospels published in this country. An "Advertisement" states that "it was also designed to print the Harmony respecting the resurrection of Christ, according to the order proposed by Townson in his Essay on the Four Gospels, and followed by Professor White in his Diatessaron; but after diligent search no copy of the Essays could be found, and it was thought inexpedient to depart from the order of Newcome, without assigning the reasons, which succeeding Harmonists have alleged for a departure. Newcome himself, who read Townson, did not think proper to alter that part of his Harmony, to which this paragraph alludes." The form of this American Newcome is 8vo, pp. xvi., xii., 424, 188. Another edition appeared the same year in 4to.

Newcome's Harmony appeared at Dublin in 1788, folio; a Harmony constructed on the basis of Le Clerc, Amsterdam, 1699, fol. Professor White, alluded to in the "Advertisement," was Joseph White, professor of the Hebrew and Arabic languages in Oxford University, and the same who published the Philoxenian (Harklensian) Syriac New Testament (Oxford, 1778–1803), and the so-called "Origenistic" Greek New Testament, with its *obeli* and asterisks (Oxford, 1798–1808). The Diatessaron passed through a number of editions in the earlier years of this century (fifth edition, Oxford, 1814, small 8vo).

Another issue of the same text appeared at Philadelphia in 1822–23, in parallel columns with an original, or revised, English Version, edited by "Abner Kneeland, minister of the First Independent Church of Christ, called Universalist, in Philadelphia;" also the same in 1823; also the Greek text alone (1822) and the author's English version by itself (1823), and perhaps each of them twice. At least, some copies of the Greek are dated 1823; which I am inclined to believe is the *true* date of both the single texts. It was "published by the Editor, No. 9 North Second Street, and sold by him—also by Abm. Small, No. 165 Chestnut Street." William Fry, often said to be the publisher, was the printer (spelled "printe" in vol. i. of the issue of 1822, but "printer" in vol. ii., as well as in both volumes of the issue of 1823). The form is a rather small 12mo, vol. i., pp. xvi. 360; vol. ii., pp. ix. 444. The Greek is printed without accents, and the Griesbach margin is omitted. It was intended by the author to supply the want of a Greek-English New Testament; a thing which he believed not to be in existence; and the printing of the Greek and English separately was an afterthought.

The first volume appeared as an experiment; with a preface containing, among other things, the Greek Alphabet, directions for pronunciation, and the declension of the article and personal pronouns. An abstract from Parkhurst's Greek Grammar is promised for the second volume, provided the work meets with sufficient encouragement—which promise is fulfilled at the end of the second volume. The long lists of errata in each volume show the editor's care and the printer's ability; but it is to be remembered that the editor, as he himself says with regret, lacked the privilege of an early classical education.[1] The whole book shows more the author's

[1] Abner Kneeland (b. 1774; d. 1844) was a Baptist clergyman, then Universalist, then Deist. He edited a Universalist periodical in Philadelphia (1821–23); the *Olive Branch*, New York; founded the *Investigator* at Boston (1832); in 1836 was tried before the Supreme Court at Boston for blasphemy. He published several other books.

sense of his own need and deficiencies than any conceit of the "self-made" man; though of course it has many of the crudities of the latter, with the common belief of the class that they shall yet light upon the royal road to learning.

The type of this Greek Testament appears to be the same as that used in the "Enchiridion of Epictetus," mentioned above as probably the first Greek book published in America, with, however, more recent forms for some of the letters intermingled. The use of the type can be traced in a series of small Greek grammars, and other books, printed in Philadelphia, by Carey, Aitken, and Fry, respectively; some of which grammars contain the Lord's Prayer and other New Testament passages in Greek, besides the Ten Commandments from the Septuagint.

The next Griesbach New Testament issued in this country was printed without either breathings or accents. This is the notorious "Emphatic Diaglott" now regularly published by the "phrenological" firm, S. R. Wells & Co., of New York. It is an astonishing edition, by reason of its high price, its mysterious name, and its other qualities. It was first published by the editor, Benjamin Wilson, at Geneva, Illinois; the issue extending over a period of seven years, ending in 1863; the whole, when afterwards bound together, bearing the date 1864. The second edition, or the first issued at once in a complete form, was published by Fowler & Wells, New York, in 1865; the editor's preface being dated 1864. Its claims are best set forth by its title: "The Emphatic Diaglott: containing the Original Greek Text of what is commonly styled the New Testament, (according to the Recension of Dr. J. J. Griesbach,) with an Interlineary Word for Word English Translation; a New Emphatic Version, based on the Interlineary Translation, on the renderings of eminent critics, and on the various readings of the Vatican Manuscript, No. 1209 in the Vatican Library. Together with Illustrative and Explanatory foot notes, and a copious selection of References; to the whole of which is added, A Valuable Alphabetical Appendix." No remarks need be made upon the style of editing, or upon either of the translations; unless it be to say that the only respectable portion of the prefatory matter is the "History of the Greek Text;" and that is not faultless. The Griesbach margin is generally omitted, except when it happens to coincide with a "Vatican Manuscript, No. 1209" reading. But as to the source of these Vatican readings, I judge from sundry indications, such as *"Εὐροχλυδων"* (Acts 27 : 14) without note of a variant, that it was some reprint of the inaccurate edition of Angelo Mai; probably that of Appleton, New York, 1859.

The form of this "Emphatic Diaglott"[1] is a 12mo, apparently; with no paging or sheet signatures, except in the Appendix, which has pp. 44. As far as I have traced this edition, it has reappeared in 1866, 1870, 1871, 1872, 1876, 1878, 1880; also the Gospel of Luke separately in 1878, in quest of patronage through the "International Sunday-School Lessons."

The last Griesbach text which I find issued in this country is a portion of an "Interlinear Translation of the Sacred Scriptures," of which the Pentateuch, Daniel, and Ezra have appeared in Hebrew and English, and the Gospels, Acts, and Apocalypse in Greek and English. The work came out in parts; at first, a Hebrew and a Greek part alternately, beginning with the Hebrew. One part was to be issued every three months. The notes, grammatical and critical, were bound up at the end of each part as it came out, but when the collected parts were bound together (the Pentateuch by itself, Daniel and Ezra each by itself, and the New Testament portions in one volume by themselves), the notes, having a separate and continuous paging, were put together at the end of the volume. The general title of the work is "Interlinear Translation of the Sacred Scriptures, with Grammatical and Critical Notes. By Dr. Leonard Tafel, New York; Dr. Rudolph L. Tafel, London; L. H. Tafel, Philadelphia." The special title of the New Testament portions is: "Interlinear Translation

---

[1] This word, I am informed, has been used as meaning *interlinear;* and therefore may not be a mistake for "Diglott." But in the book itself it is not the "interlineary" part that is "emphatic," but the other English version.

of the New Testament," etc. The New Testament portion is
issued with two different imprints; the first " Philadelphia: L.
H. Tafel, 635 Arch Street. London: David Nutt, 270,
Strand." The other issue bears the imprint " New York:
E. and J. B. Young, & Co., Cooper Union, Fourth Avenue.
London, James Speiss, 36 Bloomsbury Street." The form is
8vo, pp. viii. 730; notes, pp. 76. The text is that of Griesbach
with modifications. Besides the interlinear translation, there
is a transliteration (also interlinear) of the Greek into Roman
letters, after a fashion explained in the introductory matter.
The work bears no date, but the parts appeared at various
times in the last decade. I suspect that the actual printing
of the Hebrew and Greek was done abroad; the Hebrew, at
least, probably by Drugulin, of Leipzig. The work belongs
to the class of literary curiosities; though portions of it are
not without merit. The Greek is printed without accents.

3

V. THE STEPHANIC EDITIONS.

THE Stephanic editions are treated separately from the Mill editions, only because the phenomena in America require it. They form the next thread to be taken up in chronological order. The first of these was the edition of Peter Wilson,[1] LL.D., Professor Emeritus of Columbia College, New York. This was first published in 1822, at Hartford, Connecticut, by Oliver D. Cooke & Sons; stereotyped by Hammond Wallis, New York. In Reuss's *Bibliotheca N. T. Gr.*, p. 163 (and its "Index Editionum," p. 296), the first issue is mistakenly set down as "New York, stereotypis Hammondi Wallis. 1808." But stereotyping was not introduced into America till about 1813; and Peter Wilson was not Professor Emeritus of Columbia College till 1820; and about 1808 he must have been too busy with his *Latin Prosody* (New York, 1810) to be editing a Greek Testament. Indeed, his known labors and published works account pretty well for all his time. (See Dr.

---

[1] Peter Wilson, b. 1746, in Scotland, studied at the University of Aberdeen, removed to New York 1763, member of New Jersey Legislature 1777–83, codifier of the New Jersey laws 1783, Professor in Columbia College 1789–92 and again 1797–1820. In 1820 he was made Professor Emeritus. d. 1825. I am informed by Mr. C. J. Buckingham of Poughkeepsie, N. Y., that the late Prof. Chauncey A. Goodrich, of Yale College, actually superintended the printing of Wilson's Greek Testament, and that at the time of its publication it was commonly called "Goodrich's Greek Testament," although Goodrich's name nowhere appears in the book. Mr. Buckingham studied the first edition of this Gr. N. T. at Bacon Academy, Colchester, Connecticut, at the same time with Chief Justice Waite, in the days when sub-freshmen had to almost know the Greek Testament by heart. Professor Goodrich was a son-in-law of Noah Webster, and brother-in-law of the *last* Governor Ellsworth of Connecticut. In 1822, the same year in which he saw this Greek N. T. through the press, he published the first edition of his well-known elementary Greek grammar (Hartford, Huntington & Hopkins), whose exercises consist in great part of extracts from the Greek New Testament.

34

H. Drisler's article, *Wilson, Peter,* in Johnson's Cyclopædia.)
Moreover, Reuss had not seen an edition of 1808, nor does
he state his authority. The origin of the error is probably
to be seen on p. 137 of Reuss's *Bibliotheca*—in a confusion
for the moment with the (Scotch or) English printer, Andrew
Wilson. An index error in O'Callaghan's *American Bibles,*
p. 414, of " C. P. Wilson " for "*cura* P. Wilson," may have
added to the confusion. Reuss had seen no edition earlier
than 1829.

This edition of Wilson is a 12mo, pp. 368, with no accessory matter; but bearing on the titlepage the statement that
it is "ad exemplar Roberti Stephani accuratissime impressum." Dr. Edward Robinson had written to Reuss that " it
has no critical value, and probably Prof. Wilson did nothing
more than read the proofs." But Reuss found otherwise. He
states that out of the 56 differences of moment between the
first (1546) and third (1550) editions of R. Stephanus, Wilson
retains the reading of the first in 38 places; also that he de-
serts the latter in 22 other places. All which I have verified.
The places which Reuss gives in particular may be summar-
ized as follows: from the Complutensian New Testament, as
retained in Stephanus of 1546, to Erasmus or Elzevir, 10
places; from Erasmus, as retained by Stephanus of 1546, to
the Complutensian, 2 places; from the older Stephanus to
the later, 6 places; also, 3 places where the first three Stephanus editions agree, but Wilson leaves them all for Elzevir; and also one Erasmian reading adopted by Wilson which
occurs in neither the Stephanus nor the Elzevir editions. (See
Reuss, *Bibliotheca,* pp. 163, 164.) The places not given in
particular can be easily picked out from the lists (*idem,* pp.
50–58).[1] An examination of these variations from the Ste-

---

[1] The places specified *in particular* by Reuss are as follows: departures from
the Complutensian to Erasmus or Elzevir, Matt. 9 : 17, ἀμφότερα for ἀμφότεροι;
Matt. 26 : 52, ἀπολοῦνται for ἀποθανοῦνται; Mark 11 : 1, Βηθφαγῆ for Βηθσφαγῆ;
Matt. 24 : 31, σάλπιγγος φωνῆς for σάλπιγγος καὶ φωνῆς; 1 Pet. 2 : 21, ἡμῶν, ἡμῖν
for ὑμῶν, ὑμῖν; Luke 5 : 19, διὰ ποίας for ποίας; Matt. 19 : 9, εἰ μὴ ἐπὶ πορνείᾳ
for μὴ ἐπὶ πορνείᾳ; Matt. 21 : 1, same as Mark 11 : 1; Luke 3 : 2, ἀρχιερέων
for ἀρχιερέως; Rom. 2 : 5, omitting καὶ after ἀποκαλύψεως. Departures from
Erasmus to Complutensian: Acts 12 : 25, Σαῦλος for Παῦλος [this also in R. Ste-

phanic editions, without going any farther, will make us agree entirely with Reuss—"editionem hic quoad textum plane singularem reperi" (*idem*, p. 163).

Wilson's New Testament has had an enormous circulation, and is still in use by very many. Probably no edition was more commonly used by the mass of clergymen and students from 1823 to 1840. The editions which have come to my knowledge are the following: Hartford, Oliver D. Cooke & Sons, 1822, 1825, 1827, 1829; Philadelphia, Towar & Hogan, 1829, 1831; Philadelphia, Towar, Hogan & Thompson, 1833; Philadelphia, Haswell, Barrington, & Haswell (with other firms, one in Pittsburgh), 1838; Philadelphia, Ed. Barrington & Geo. D. Haswell, not dated, but issued at least as early as 1851 (known by a printer's—not binder's—error in transposing pages 142, 143 with pages 242, 243), and the same corrected, giving the publishers' place of business at 293 Market Street, also again without date, giving the publishers' place at 27 North Sixth Street (one of these latter issued in 1854); Philadelphia, Lippincott, Grambo, & Co., 1854; Philadelphia, J. B. Lippincott, & Co., 1858, 1859, 1860; Philadelphia, Claxton, Remsen, & Haffelfinger, 1870, 1880.

Following Wilson, in the same family, and next also in order of time, comes one of the most remarkable pieces of book-making to be found in modern sacred literature. This professes to be John Leusden's, with the Latin version of Arias Montanus; also to have Leusden's 1900 select verses marked with a *, besides his † and ‡, for their several purposes. The title is evidently copied from the Leusden edition of Long

---

phanus, 1551]; 2 Tim. 4 : 13, φελόνην for φαιλόνην. Leaves R. Stephanus 1546 for a later R. Stephanus : Mark 8 : 34, ἐλθεῖν for ἀκολουθεῖν ; Mark 14 : 32, ἕως προσεύξωμαι for ἕως προσεύξομαι ; Mark 8 : 13, εἰς τὸ πλοῖον for εἰς πλοῖον ; 1 Cor. 15 : 33, χρῆσθ᾽ [sic] for χρηστά ; Phil. 2 : 1, εἴ τινα for εἴ τις ; Rev. 10 : 4, μὴ ταῦτα γράψῃς for μὴ ταῦτα γράφῃς. Leaves Stephanus for Elzevir : Matt. 21 : 7, ἐπεκάθισαν for ἐπεκάθισεν [this also Stephanus 1551]; Coloss. 1 : 2, Κολοσσαῖς for Κολασσαῖς ; 1 Pet. 3 : 21, ᾧ καὶ ἡμᾶς for ὃ καὶ ἡμᾶς. Erasmian unknown to Stephanus or Elzevir, Mark 7 : 26, Συροφοινίκισσα for Συροφοίνισσα. For the differences *not* particularly mentioned, *i. e.*, the 38 first mentioned above, see Reuss's lists (*idem*, pp. 50–54).

(New York, 1821),[1] so as to have an orthodox and market-catching title for a Greek-Latin edition. It is a 12mo, pp. 775, Greek and Latin in parallel columns, and first published at New York, in 1824, by Collins and Hannay, stereotyped by Hammond Wallis & Co. Reuss (*idem*, pp. 128, 129), without seeing it, had noted it as a genuine Leusden, on the authority of the late Rev. Dr. C. P. Krauth. But the fact is otherwise, as Reuss would have known had he seen that edition; for he did detect it in the repetition of 1858. So far from being a Leusden, of the Elzevir family, it is nothing but a Wilson, from plates that the stereotyper (who two years before had stereotyped Wilson) could easily furnish, and apparently did; with scarcely more alteration than to cut them in half length-wise, so as to fit the pieces alongside the Latin column. Wilson, however, is altered in one place, viz., by inserting the verse Luke 17 : 36, so as to accommodate the Latin and tally better with the real Leusden editions. But besides the general falsehood of the title, these minor statements about the 1900 select verses marked with a *, and the †, and the ‡, are false likewise. No trace whatever of any of them appears in the text.

O'Callaghan (*Amer. Bibles*, p. 368), first finding this book in its issue of 1858, unsuspectingly and innocently remarks that it inverts the order of the verses Matt. 23 : 13, 14; not knowing that this inversion was one of the distinguishing characteristics of a family of texts different from Leusden.

The deceptive character of this edition is equalled only by the extent of its success. The first spurious Leusden of 1675 (see p. 23, note) furnishes no adequate parallel. It is still in print, apparently from the very same plates as at first, and still finds a ready market. I am informed by the Philadelphia booksellers that this edition, together with Wilson's and the Polymicrian, are the ones which the new crop of students,

---

[1] Long was employed as a printer by Collins & Hannay for other publications. The names of Collins, Hannay, Long, and Dean all appear on the titlepage in some books. For instance, the fifth American edition of Valpy's Elements of Greek Grammar, with additions, etc., by Charles Anthon, New York, 1825, bears as its imprint, "Evert Duyckinck, George Long, Collins & Co., and Collins & Hannay. W. E. Dean, printer."

every autumn, chiefly purchase. It may readily be recognized by a mistake in the title to Matthew, where an *O* still holds the place of a *θ*, as it has done from the beginning.

The other issues which have come to my knowledge are: New York, Collins & Hannay, 1831; New York, B. & S. Collins, 1835; New York, Collins, Keese, & Co. (W. E. Dean, printer), 1836, 1838; New York, W. E. Dean, also Collins, 1840; New York, W. E. Dean, 1844, 1849, 1851, 1852, 1853; Philadelphia, Lippincott, Grambo, & Co., 1855; Philadelphia, J. B. Lippincott & Co., 1858, 1859, 1860, 1863, 1865, 1875, 1876, 1878, 1880, 1882. Wilson under false colors has had a circulation rather more extended than Wilson under the true.

Whatever doubt may be entertained respecting the propriety of classing the two preceding publications among the Stephanic editions, none can exist with regard to the issue of Dr. F. H. A. Scrivener's convenient manual, issued by Henry Holt, & Co., at New York, 1879. It is bound up with the Rev. Thomas Sheldon Green's revision of Greenfield's Lexicon. Both are impressions of the English plates.

Scrivener's Manual, as is well known, is a reprint (at the Cambridge University Press, England, 16mo, pp. viii. 598) of the third edition (1550) of Robert Stephens, with footnotes showing the different readings of noted critical editors, and a different type in the text to mark the variant places. It first appeared in 1859, and has reached at least its ninth edition; those of 1873 and later having been considerably revised —the later ones chiefly by substituting actual Beza readings for the false ones in the earlier editions. The authority for these readings Scrivener gives in the earlier editions as "Bezae 1565;" but in the edition of 1873, after his errors had been pointed out by Dr. Ezra Abbot in 1872, he changed it to "Bezae 1565. (Lond.)." In the edition of 1877 it is again simply "Bezae 1565," dropping the "(Lond.);" as the errors had been now corrected (but not entirely, however, and with some new ones committed) in the stereotype plates. A comparison of the earlier and later Scrivener editions with his "list of those places, in which our translation agrees with

Beza's New Testament against that of Stephens," in his *Supplement to the Authorized Version of the English N. T.* (London, 1845), pp. 7, 8 (compare the foot-note, p. 8), discloses a few indications that his collation employed in the earlier editions was made at least as long ago as 1845; and it is not improbable that either a false titlepage or his own memory has served him a bad turn. At all events, the text which he used for those earlier editions of his Greek New Testament was quite different from any Beza; and it will puzzle the most acute bibliographer either to find a London Beza of 1565 or to account for its existence. In the third (1883) edition of Scrivener's *Plain Introduction* (p. 440, note 2), he says of this hypothetical book: "It is doubtless an unauthorized and very poor reprint in quarto of the edition of 1556." But the edition of 1556 contained no Greek text, but only Latin. And the supposition that it was a *quarto* excludes the suggestion (made to me by one of Dr. Scrivener's learned countrymen) that the book was an actual Geneva impression with a London imprint. But this suggestion is inconsistent with the textual phenomena as well.

A professed reprint from this edition of Scrivener is a work with the following title: "The Epistle to the Romans, in Greek, in which the Text of Robert Stephens, Third Edition, is compared with the Text of the Elzevirs, Lachmann, Alford, Tregelles, Tischendorf, and Westcott, and with the chief uncial and cursive MSS., together with references to the New Testament Grammars of Winer and Buttmann. By Henry A. Buttz, professor of New Testament Exegesis in Drew Theological Seminary. New York: Nelson & Phillips. Cincinnati: Hitchcock & Walden. 1876." It is an 8vo, pp. 42; and contains Scrivener's text and margin, with a compilation, in the shape of foot-notes, from Alford and others. It was "intended as the beginning of an edition of the entire Greek Testament with textual and grammatical references;" but the work has not been continued. Its comparisons with Westcott appear to be based on so much of Westcott & Hort's text as appeared in Dr. C. J. Vaughan's Romans (London, Macmillan

& Co., 4th ed., 1873); and the grammatical references closely correspond with Professor J. H. Thayer's indexes in his translations of Winer and Buttmann. A second edition of Prof. Buttz's work appeared in 1877, and a third in 1879; the same place and publishers.

VI. THE KNAPP EDITIONS.

KNAPP's text was the next to make its appearance; in the shape of a Harmony of the Gospels constructed by Dr. Edward Robinson "in the general order of Le Clerc and Newcome," and with Newcome's notes; published at Andover, by Gould & Newman (also New York, Lord, Leavitt, & Co.), in 1834; 8vo, pp. xxviii. 328. It has also Knapp's various readings; and two appendixes, giving, severally, Dr. Benson's and Dr. Lardner's manner of harmonizing the accounts of Christ's resurrection. Knapp's fourth edition[1] is apparently the text here followed. Knapp's text differed somewhat from Griesbach, but seems to have inserted only one reading peculiar to himself; the other variants coming from other less known editors, among whom Mace (1729, published anonymously— too much censured in his own time, and too much neglected later) seems to be chiefly followed. Knapp's editions were published at Halle in 1797, 1813, 1824, 1829, 1840, besides a Greek-German one at Berlin in 1837. The second and third are identical; and so, again, are the fourth and fifth. The fourth edition has been very extensively imported and used in America; and a copy is to be seen in the library of almost every scholar who has passed middle life. It is still a pleasant book to use.

Knapp's text again appeared in "The Student's New Testament," edited by R. B. Patton, and published by Charles Starr, New York, 1835. It was printed on ruled writing-paper with very wide margins (the edition being intended for

---

[1] That is, the fourth genuine Knapp. The edition published by Valpy, London, 1824, though called "fourth edition," is really an altered reprint of the third.

note-taking students), and so arranged that a verse always ends at the foot of a page. Otherwise this edition keeps Knapp's paragraphs, also his spaces to mark sub-paragraphs (like Bengel's before Knapp, and Westcott & Hort's more recently); with his other conveniences and accessory matter. It has also a preface by Patton. It is a reproduction of Knapp's fourth edition entire, " with the exception of the Latin arguments of the chapters, at the bottom of the page." This edition, stereotyped, was issued again at New York by J. C. Riker, in 1845 (styled falsely " Editio Prima Americana Stereotypa " on the titlepage), and by the same again, without date. It was to be had either separately or bound up with the English Old Testament, printed on the same ruled paper with broad margins. The whole formed " The Student's Bible." It was a large 4to, the New Testament having pp. xix., foll. 234, pp. 235–248. In some copies of each issue, the leaves containing the text are printed upon one side only, and that portion has the folios (only) numbered. But other copies of each issue have both sides printed upon, and, of course, all the pages (248) numbered. In the latter form the book has scarcely half the thickness of the other.

VII. THE BLOOMFIELD EDITIONS.

THE next family to appear were the Bloomfields. The American edition of Bloomfield (2 vols. 8vo, pp. xxxii. 597, 631) appeared at Boston in 1837, under the superintendence of Moses Stuart, and with a preface by him. The titlepage reads as follows: "*Ἡ ΚΑΙΝΗ ΔΙΑΘΗΚΗ*. The Greek Testament, with English Notes, critical, philological, and exegetical, partly selected and arranged from the best commentators, ancient and modern, but chiefly original. The whole being especially adapted to the use of Academical Students, Candidates for the Sacred Office, and Ministers; though also intended as a manual edition for the use of theological readers in general. By the Rev. S. T. Bloomfield, D. D., F. S. A., vicar of Bisbrooke, Rutland. First American from the second London edition. In two volumes. . . . Boston: Published by Perkins and Marvin. Philadelphia: Henry Perkins. 1837." The "Preface to the American Edition" is dated "October 1st, 1836," and the work is said to have actually appeared in that year. Some copies insert, between the Boston and Philadelphia publishers' names, the words "New York: Gould and Newman."

It is not an easy matter to trace or to enumerate all the reissues. They are all from the same plates, which ever since the dissolution of the Boston firm, about 1842, have been in the possession of Henry Perkins, of Philadelphia, who was a brother of Benjamin Perkins, of the firm of Perkins & Marvin. The most diligent search has failed to discover any copy of the second, third, or fourth edition; or any edition after the fifth until we come to the fourteenth. Whether editions with these undiscovered numbers ever existed or not, I am unable, nor is the owner of the stereotype plates able, to tell. The suggestion naturally presents itself that the American publishers counted the English editions as members of the series; but there are several difficulties in the way of that explanation, one of which difficulties is to determine the method—whether based on fact or on fiction—which could have been followed in such counting. Not only the American but the English Bloomfields are a vexation to the bibliographer.

Besides the changes in the imprint, the title appears in a somewhat abbreviated form in the later editions. The subsequent issues which I have traced are the following: fifth American edition, Philadelphia, Perkins & Purves, 1843; the same, Philadelphia, H. Perkins, Boston, Benjamin Perkins, 1846; the same, Boston, Perkins, Philadelphia, H. Perkins, 1848; the same, Philadelphia, H. Perkins, Boston, Perkins & Marvin [sic], 1848; the same, Philadelphia, H. Perkins, Boston, Benjamin Perkins, 1848; the same, Philadelphia, Clark & Hesser, 1854; the same, Philadelphia, H. C. Peck & Theo. Bliss, 1854 (making thus far two forms of the " first American edition " and seven forms of the " fifth American edition "); Philadelphia, Lippincott, 1856, edition-number not known; 14th edition, Philadelphia, Lippincott, 1868, 1869, 1870. I have also learned that several issues appeared between 1856 and 1868, all bearing the imprint of Lippincott, Philadelphia, but their dates and edition-numbers I have been unable to ascertain.

As to text, this book is to be considered as an altered Mill, notwithstanding its bracketed insertions in the text from various sources. It is more noteworthy as a *multum in parvo* commentary (of high ecclesiastical color) than as a text, but it has little critical merit of the desirable sort. Its mention of the readings of the MSS. is made in a manner so loose and careless, that the natural expansion thereof in the ninth edition (London, 1855) results in many statements wholly imaginary; such, for example, as citing the Vatican MS. in a portion of the New Testament where that MS. is lacking.[1] (See,

---

[1] That, however, is scarcely equal to the Lord Bishop of London's remark in *The Speaker's Commentary* on 1 Tim. 3 : 16 (N. T. vol. iii. p. 780): " The Vati-

for example, the note on 2 Timothy 2 : 3, where this is done with not only that MS. but others also. Also, note on 2 Corinthians 5 : 12, where a pretended quotation is similarly made from the Alexandrine MS.—which lacks 2 Cor. 4 : 13 to 12 : 6.) The first original Bloomfield appeared at London in 1832 ; the second, much amended and improved, in 1836. It is this second edition which is reproduced in the American edition. But all the Bloomfield editions are as nearly worthless as it is possible for such a large and laborious work to be. It is not that they do not contain an abundance of good matter, but the good is so hopelessly mixed up with the bad and the inaccurate, that they are not fit for the learner, nor worth sifting by the learned.

Bloomfield's minor edition (London, several editions between 1840 and 1860), 12mo, was imported by Lippincott, and is said to be sometimes seen with their imprint, but I have seen it with their name only on the back of the bound volume. I do not know that this edition has ever been reprinted in America. (For the curious matter of its readings—their alleged agreement with and actual difference from the larger editions—see Reuss, *Biblioth. N. T. Gr.*, p. 238.)

can MS. cannot be appealed to [*i. e.* as to whether the reading is ὅς, or θεός], because the jealousy of Rome has prevented accurate collation, and the edition published by Cardinal Mai proves to be not so much a faithful reproduction of the MS. as an edition of the New Testament grounded upon it." The Lord Bishop surely ought to know that the Vatican MS. does not contain the Pastoral Epistles.

IX. THE HAHN EDITIONS.

ROBINSON'S Hahn,[1] the next in order, is almost too well known to need description; but it is rapidly being crowded out by later critical works, and may cease before long to be familiar. It is a reprint of Augustus Hahn's recension of the edition of John Augustus Henry Tittmann; differing from Hahn's edition of 1840 (Leipzig, Tauchnitz) only by an "Advertisement" of Dr. Edward Robinson's dated May 10, 1842, and by giving the "Notices of the Principal Manuscripts and other Helps for the Criticism of the Greek Text of the New Testament" in English, instead of Latin. It retains the marginal notes of the original, which consist of various readings of other critical editors, with parallel Scripture references. The address of Tittmann to the kind reader ("L. B. S."), dated Leipzig, 25 Nov., 1819, and that of Hahn, dated Wratislaw, 12 May, 1840, are retained in Latin. The book is a 12mo, pp. xxviii. 508.

This edition, called "Editio Stereotypa Americana" on the titlepage, first appeared in 1842, with three different forms of the imprint, two of them dated. The imprint of the undated issue was "New York: Leavitt & Allen," and this was often reissued. The others bore the imprint of "New York: Leavitt & Trow; Boston: Crocker and Brewster," and "Boston: Crocker & Brewster. New York: Leavitt & Trow," respectively. That is, they bore the same names, but in reversed order. The other dated issues, as far as I have been able to trace them, are the following: New York, Leavitt & Trow; Boston, Crocker & Brewster, 1845; and another issue by the same, the same year, *in 8vo;* New York, Leavitt & Allen, 1854, 1855, 1857;

---

[1] All the American Hahn texts are the *earlier.* The later Hahn text, 1861, etc., has not been reprinted here.

New York, Appleton, 1866, 1867, 1868, 1870, 1872, 1875, 1880. The book had a circulation as respectable as it was extensive, but the day of its preference as a critical edition has long been passed.

Robinson's Harmony (8vo, pp. xx. 235) naturally belongs to the same text. This, Robinson's own arrangement and Hahn's text, was published at Boston by Crocker & Brewster, in 1845. A Revised edition, differing from the first chiefly in the schedule of events in the Passion Week, was issued by the same publishers at the same place, 1851, 1853, 1857, 1859, 1862, 1865, 1872; also Boston, Houghton, Osgood, & Co., 1879; Boston, Houghton, Mifflin, & Co., 1879, 1882. In its time, this Harmony easily distanced all others in America in popularity, if not in merit. It was the lineal successor and descendant, so to speak, of the first Harmony published in America; and the memory of its author is still a power in its circulation. But the progress of Biblical science does not stop with any one generation or its acquisitions.

Another specimen of the Hahn text appears in the " Collectanea Evangelica," or selections from the Gospels, with a passage or two from the Acts, arranged in "chronological order" so as to form a connected history of the principal events in the life and ministry of Christ. Its compiler is N. C. Brooks, A.M., then principal of the high school in Baltimore, afterwards LL.D., and president of the (Methodist) Baltimore Female College. The " Collectanea " was intended as a school-book,[1] and is provided with notes and a lexicon. It is a rather small 16mo, pp. 210, published at Baltimore, 1847, two editions the same year, by Cushing & Brother, also Sorin & Ball at Philadelphia; third edition, New York, A. S. Barnes & Co., also Cincinnati, H. W. Derby & Co., 1849. The stereotype plates were made in New York.

---

[1] One of a series of school-books edited by the compiler; a series recommended by Edgar A. Poe, then editor of the *Broadway Journal*, N. Y. His recommendation is printed in the fly-leaves of the first two editions of the " Collectanea."

In 1871 this book was again issued from the same plates, but with a new titlepage, a new name, a new copyright note, a new dedication to a different person, and a shortened preface. This time it is the " Harmonia Evangelica: a Greek Harmony of the Four Gospels;" but in the Dedication it is called also a " Monotessaron." It was issued at Philadelphia, by Claxton, Remsen, and Haffelfinger. The sub-title on the first page of the text, and the running titles at the top of the pages, are changed to correspond.

To the same Hahn text conform also Owen's edition of the Acts of the Apostles,[1] with notes and vocabulary; 12mo, pp. xii. 276, New York, Leavitt, 1850, 1852, 1856; New York, Appleton, 1869, 1875, 1876, 1882; and chiefly also Professor Samuel H. Turner's[2] editions of several Epistles, with English translation, and a commentary. These were, Hebrews, pp. viii. 186, New York, Stanford & Swords, 1852, and again

---

[1] John Jason Owen, D.D., LL.D., b. 1803 at Colebrook, Connecticut; graduated at Middlebury College, Vermont, 1829, and at Andover Theological Seminary, 1831; president of Cornelius Institute, New York; professor of Latin and Greek in New York Free Academy, 1848, and its vice-principal in 1853; vice-president of the College of the City of New York, 1866; d. at New York, 1869. His editions of Xenophon's Anabasis and Cyropædia, of the Iliad, the Odyssey, and Thucydides (Peloponnesian War), his Greek Reader, and his Commentary on the Gospels, were familiar to most American students not many years ago, and have not yet gone entirely out of use. It is of this edition of the Acts that "J. H. W." thus speaks in *Mc Clintock & Strong's Cyclopædia*, vol. vii. p. 496: "It was a frequent comment of Prof. Owen's that theological students were unable to combine the study of Greek and of the Bible at the same time, to remedy which he finally translated the Acts of the Apostles into Greek, appending a dictionary of the words in the same language." Dr. Owen's scholarly work has, however, met with a very competent and sensible, as well as wide, appreciation.

[2] Samuel Hulbeart Turner, D.D., b. at Philadelphia, 1790; graduated at the University of Pennsylvania 1807; professor in the General (Episcopal) Theological Seminary, New York, 1818–20, and again 1821 till his death; also professor of Hebrew in Columbia College from 1831; d. at New York, 1861. Besides the works here noticed, Professor Turner was the author of a Companion to the Book of Genesis, Biographical Notices of Distinguished Rabbis, Parallel References Illustrative of the New Testament, The Gospels according to the Ammonian sections and the Tables of Eusebius (translated from the Oxford Greek edition of 1805), and several other works of kindred character and merit.

1855; Romans, pp. xvi. 252, New York, Stanford & Swords, 1853, again, 1855, and again, New York, Randolph, 1859; Galatians, pp. xiii. 98, New York, Dana & Co., 1856; Ephesians, pp. xix. 198, New York, Dana & Co., 1856; all in 8vo. All these are known as works of high character. Turner's works deal largely with questions of textual criticism; many pages being almost wholly occupied in their discussion.

4

X. MISCELLANEOUS.

In 1830 appeared "The Gospel of St. John, in Greek and English, interlined and literally translated: with a transposition of the words into their due order of construction; and a dictionary defining and parsing them: principally designed for the use of schools. By E. Friederici. New York: published·for the author, by G. F. Bunce, 224 Cherry St." 16mo, pp. 176, 2 leaves. I have had no opportunity to examine its text.

In 1861 was published at Philadelphia, by Charles Desilver, an edition of the Gospel of John, 12mo, pp. 292, edited by George William Heilig, containing an "interlinear and analytical translation," and a great deal of accessory matter. This was one of the "Hamiltonian System" of schoolbooks, as improved by Thomas Clark. One-half of the book seems to be a reprint of James Hamilton's *Gospel of John in Greek*, etc., fifth edition, London, 1847; and the other half matter compiled by Heilig from well-known sources, which he states in full. On the right hand page is the text with the interlinear translation; and this portion comprises the reprinted matter. The left hand page contains the text again, alongside of the Common English version (American Bible Society's edition of 1852) and the Roman Catholic (from Cummiskey's Bible, Philadelphia, 1840), with Scripture references in the outer and lower margins and grammatical notes at the foot. The grammatical and historical notes are taken from Rev. Dr. C. P. Krauth's translation of Tholuck's *Commentary on the Gospel of John* (Philadelphia, 1879). At the end are eight pages of "critical annotations." The Greek text is professedly that of Theile, editio stereotypa, Leipzig, Tauchnitz, 1858.

Theile's text was professedly based on Knapp; but it is quite a different affair from Knapp, having a very large element derived from recent critical editors, among whom Griesbach, Lachmann, Hahn, and Tischendorf hold the chief place. Theile's New. Testament (*editio stereotypa*) is the one which replaced Tittmann in the familiar series of Tauchnitz classics. It has been "usu in Germania tritissima," and not altogether unknown in America.

Tischendorf's text (ed. viii. *crit. maj.*) is adopted in the Harmony of the Gospels by Professor Frederic Gardiner, D.D., of the Berkeley Divinity School, Middletown, Connecticut. It is an 8vo, published at Andover, by Warren F. Draper, 1871, 1872, 1873, 1875, 1876 (revised ed., pp. lv. 268, 64), 1879, 1880. This work has come into quite general use, and has in a measure superseded and displaced Robinson's Harmony; its differences from the latter having generally a basis of later investigation. It contains several features which add greatly to the convenience of a work of the sort, such as giving Old Testament references in the original Hebrew, and in the Septuagint Greek when necessary, and, especially, a table which shows at a glance the arrangement of events adopted in the best known or the most widely used Harmonies. Appended is an excellent summary of the "Principles of Textual Criticism," with a "Graphic Table of New Testament Uncials," which last exhibits to the eye at a glance the uncial record of every passage in the New Testament.

In 1879, but without date, was issued "A | CRITICAL AND DOCTRINAL COMMENTARY | upon the | EPISTLE OF ST. PAUL TO THE ROMANS. | By | WILLIAM G. T. SHEDD, D.D., | Roosevelt Professor of Systematic Theology in Union | Theological Seminary, New York. | NEW YORK: CHARLES SCRIBNER'S SONS, | 743 and 745 Broadway." 8vo, pp. viii. 439. The author says (Preface, p. v.): "I have adopted

the text of Lachmann, with such modifications, chiefly from
Tischendorf, as would probably have been made by Lachmann, if he had had access to those manuscripts that have
been brought to light by the industry and skill of Tischendorf." Reasons for adopting this or that reading of the text
are carefully, but briefly, given in the notes; sometimes ex-
plaining a retention of Lachmann's reading, as that of ἔχομεν
in chap. 5 : 1. This reading (preferred also by the American
Committee of Revision of the English New Testament) is
retained chiefly " for dogmatic reasons," the evidence being
otherwise deemed sufficient. The reading of Lachmann's earlier edition (1831) is ἔχωμεν; that of his second (larger edition, 2d vol. 1850), ἔχομεν.[1]

The rest of the list seems to be made up of reprints of
European editions, or of editions printed in Europe, but bearing the name and place of an American publisher.

The 8vo edition of Cardinal Angelo Mai's New Testament
after the Vatican Manuscript (the Leipzig reprint for London
booksellers) was reissued in New York by D. Appleton &
Co., in 1859, from the same (German or) English plates. An
edition is said to have been issued, also, with the imprint of
Warren F. Draper, of Andover; but Mr. Draper is not sure
about it himself. He intended to have one, and took some
steps to obtain it, but thinks that he contented himself with
those which bear Appleton's imprint. The foreign issue bears
the imprint of Williams & Norgate, London and Edinburgh,
and D. Nutt, London.

B. H. Cowper's edition of the Codex Alexandrinus, with
the defects of that MS. supplied from Küster's Mill, published
at London, but actually printed by B. G. Teubner at Leipzig,
is also to be mentioned here. It bears the imprint: "Londini

[1] Tischendorf (*N. T. Gr.*, ed. viii. *crit. maj.*, tom. ii., p. 385, note) says, Lachmann "mutavit autem lectionem quum ignoraret B eiusdem [ἔχωμεν] testem
esse." Lachmann's own note in his larger ed. (tom. ii., p. 269) is : " εχομεν
BGς, εχωμεν *ACΛ f g v ;*" an error which must, at that date, have arisen from
ignorance only, and not from lack of diligence.

venumdant Williams & Norgate, et D. Nutt; Edinburgæ, Williams & Norgate. New York, B. Westermann & Soc." It is dated 1860. 8vo, pp. xi. 503.

The Critical Greek-English New Testament of Bagster (text of Scholz, with various readings from Griesbach, Stephens 1550, Beza 1598, Elzevir 1633), 16mo, pp. [vi.] 624, has appeared with the imprint of Wiley, New York, in 1859, 1868, 1877, 1880, 1882, 1883, and perhaps other dates, besides many issues without date.[1] Other issues bear the imprint of Lippincott, Philadelphia; generally, if not always, undated. Some copies bear the imprints of both Wiley and Lippincott; and of late years, as well as sometimes earlier, the name of Bagster is generally omitted from the titlepage of the copies sent to America. Many, if not all, of these impressions without Bagster's name, were actually printed abroad, though the paper of some issues looks as if it were American. They are sometimes bound up with Bagster's (reprint of E. Schmidt's) Greek Concordance, but generally with the New Testament Lexicon of William Greenfield as revised by the Rev. Thomas Sheldon Green, M. A.; and not infrequently with both these additions.

This edition has the merit of accurately reproducing the text of Scholz; a quality which is sometimes wrongly attributed to the Bloomfield editions. A greater merit, however, consists in its various readings; though its popularity is chiefly due to its clear print, its convenient form, and its bilingual character. The original Scholz was published at Leipzig, by Fleischer, in two large quarto volumes, dated 1830 and 1836, respectively. The editor, Dr. Johann Martin Augustin Scholz, was a theological professor in the Catholic university at Bonn, and was an indefatigable and successful collector of critical

---

[1] My last inquiry of the New York publishers about recent issues of this book received the reply that their "editions of the Greek Testaments are from Bagster and Sons' stereo. plates, and the date in our editions (Gk. & Eng.) refer only to the time of a new printing." I have generally found that, kind and courteous as publishers have been to communicate information, it is generally impossible for them to furnish the dates of all their issues, except at an expense of time and trouble which it would be unreasonable to ask.

material. But his *text* has little merit, nor has it ever met with favor at the hands of critical scholars, except in Protestant England during a period of great critical blindness and pietistic prejudice. The critical notes of Scholz generally appropriate Griesbach outright when there is opportunity; once (see note on 1 Timothy 3 : 16) in such a manner as inadvertently to claim the authorship of Griesbach's *Symbolæ Criticæ*. And he is notoriously careless and inaccurate.

A very great number of editions of Bishop C. J. Ellicott's text and commentary, of several of the Epistles of Paul, have been issued, both separately and in sets, by Warren F. Draper at Andover, at various times from 1860 to 1882. Galatians and Ephesians were also issued, each by itself, by [Warren F.] Draper and Halliday at Boston, in 1866, but with the date 1867. The separate volumes issued by Draper were the following: Galatians, 1860, 1864, 1865, 1866, 1870, 1876, 1879; Ephesians, 1862, 1863, 1865, 1866, 1876, 1879; Thessalonians, 1864, 1865, 1876; Philippians, Colossians, and Philemon, 1865, 1871, 1876, 1882; Pastoral Epistles, 1865, 1876, 1881; the whole set, 1865, 1868, 1871, 1878, 1879, 1880. The successive editions were generally revised up to the latest available English improvements.

Of the original Ellicott's text and Commentary, the early editions appeared in England with the following dates: Galatians, 1854, 1859, 1863; Ephesians, 1855, 1859, 1864; Philippians, Colossians, Philemon, 1857, 1861, 1865; Thessalonians, 1858, 1862; Pastoral Epistles, 1861, 1864. These have been repeatedly followed by revised editions, almost down to the present date.

The first volume (Gospels) of Alford's Greek Testament was issued by the Harpers, New York, 1859, 8vo; the entire work by Lee & Shepard, Boston, 1871, and repeatedly. The first Alford appeared in London in successive parts, from 1849 to 1859.[1] The original of the first edition by Lee and Shep-

---

[1] In enumerating the editions of Alford's Gr. N. T., the most accurate method, if not the only proper one, is to consider each volume as a work by itself. As

ard (at least, of its first volume) was the "fourth edition," and likewise appeared at London in parts, dated respectively 1859, 1860, 1861, and 1862. The principal part of the work has passed through six different editions, each with its revisions and corrections, and some of it through a seventh; the last being stopped by Dean Alford's death (January 12, 1871). It was then printed as a "new edition," and probably stereotyped, as the forms of movable type had been kept standing during the author's lifetime. The American editions of Lee and Shepard have been only the English sheets. Their issues of 1874, 1875, 1877 (except vol. iv.), were styled "seventh edition," but (vol. iv. of 1877, with) those of 1878 and later were called "new edition." So far as I have traced these editions, they appeared as follows: 6th edition, 1871, 1872, 1873; 7th edition, 1874, 1875, 1877; "new edition," 1878, 1880, 1881, 1883.

The edition-numbers of any given date are not always the same in all the volumes or parts. For example, of Lee and Shepard's edition of 1873, volumes i. and ii. are called "sixth edition," and have Dean Alford's "Advertisement to the Sixth Edition;" volume iii. is called "fifth edition," and volume iv. "fourth edition;" each having the corresponding author's "Advertisement." Harper's edition of 1859, above-mentioned, has Dean Alford's "Advertisement to the Third Edition."

This work has been much esteemed by various classes of students; and its general value, its critical merit, and its high scholarship, are beyond question. But one who uses it without being very careful to verify his references will not infrequently be misled, and sometimes grossly.

The abridged edition of Alford, by B. H. Alford, was issued in 1869 with the imprint of Lippincott, Philadelphia. Its titlepage reads as follows: "Dean Alford's Greek Testament with English Notes (Intended for the upper forms of schools

far as I have ascertained, the following are the dates of the first appearance of the successive editions of each volume: vol. i., 1849, 1854, 1856, 1859, 1863, 1868, 1874; vol. ii., 1852, 1855, 1857, 1860, 1865, 1871, 1876; vol. iii., 1856, 1861, 1862, 1865, 1871; vol. iv., parts 1 and 2, 1859, 1862, 1866, 1871. I think this list is complete.

and for pass-men at the Universities) Abridged by Bradley H. Alford, M. A., Vicar of Leavenheath, Colchester; Late Scholar of Trinity College, Cambridge. J. B. Lippincott & Co., Philadelphia; Rivingtons, London, Oxford, and Cambridge; Deighton, Bell, & Co., Cambridge, 1869." 12mo, pp. xxvii. 644, and 2 pages of "Corrigenda." Other copies, apparently imported in sheets, bear Lippincott's name on the back of the binding, but lack his imprint.

And last, Westcott and Hort's Greek New Testament has been issued by the Harpers, at New York, from duplicate English plates; vol. i. in 1881, and vol. ii. in 1882. The work is an 8vo; vol. i., pp. xc. 580; vol. ii., pp. xxxi. 324, 188. The first volume has a valuable "Introduction to the American Edition," by Philip Schaff, D. D., LL.D., professor in the Union Theological Seminary, New York, and president of the American Bible Revision Committee. With the exception of about four pages which deal specially with the peculiarities of this edition, Dr. Schaff's Introduction might be read and studied as an introduction to the Greek New Testament in general. It contains more matter, much more condensed, and much more readable, than most treatises which attempt to cover similar ground.

As to the character of the Greek text itself, it represents the most thorough application of advanced science, and, as a whole, the most recent attainments in textual criticism. If it fails anywhere, it is in too rigid adherence to certain rules of accepting testimony; or, perhaps we may say, in carrying the application of certain chief and extremely important rules into cases where other rules should govern. But even so, the margin and appendix lay the principal alternatives before the reader.

But as an edition of the New Testament *to read*, no edition was ever printed which does so much to help the reader's understanding through the eye. The means by which this has been accomplished are too numerous and skillful to describe at length here. Of published texts, moreover (except perhaps the editions of Scrivener and

Palmer respectively, which are designed to exhibit, the one the Greek text of the Common English Version with the variations of the Revised, the other the Greek text of the Revised Version with the variations of the Common; together with the latest American Polymicrian), no edition approaches so nearly the readings adopted in the Revised English Version.

The second volume is the most important addition of recent times to the mass of works on New Testament criticism. It differs from its predecessors chiefly in the systematizing of critical material and in the elaboration and application of critical principles. The whole work is indispensable to scholars; though it does not supersede the larger storehouses of material, whether treatises, or editions of the New Testament. Yet some of its extended discussions, as, for example, that on the twelve verses at the end of the Gospel of Mark (pp. 28 ff. of *Notes on Select Readings*), efficiently supplement, and sometimes supersede, all that is to be found in the more copious works.

The text of vol. i., with the Introduction of Dr. Schaff, was also issued by the same publishers, interleaved with the Revised English Version, in 1882. It contains, among other things, a list of the Greek readings where the Revisers of the English Version differ in judgment from Westcott and Hort.

Before publishing, Westcott and Hort issued successive "confidential" instalments of the Greek text to the members of the Company of Revisers of the English New Testament, and to a few other scholars. The Gospels, with a temporary preface of 28 pages, were thus issued in July, 1871; the Acts in February, 1873; the Catholic Epistles in December, 1873; the Pauline Epistles in February, 1875; and the Apocalypse in December, 1876. Thus this edition had almost unexampled opportunities for attaining correctness in detail; and its typographical accuracy is quite exceptional. A few misprints in the first impressions, *e.g.*, ὡμῶν for ὑμῶν, Matthew 10:6, have been corrected. Both volumes of the first published edition bear date 1881. They were printed at the University Press at Cambridge, and bear the imprint " Cambridge and London | Macmillan and Co."

The University Presses of Oxford and Cambridge have issued many a work of which the English nation is justly proud, and for which the Christian world is grateful; but since the noble edition of Mill, no work of either press has done more to bring back from Germany to England her former pre-eminence in New Testament critical study. In the greatest contribution to that end hitherto, not to say the greatest work of this nature in England for a century and a half, the University Presses had scarcely any share. That was the work of Dr. Samuel Prideaux Tregelles, accomplished in the face of the wealth and power that mostly clung to blind tradition; in toil almost single-handed, in privation, and later with the disadvantage of failing eyes, under far too much misappreciation, perverse opposition, and even obloquy— until his mustard seed had grown to a great herb in which the fowls of the air might build their nests.[1]   But had Tregelles lived to see the present day, no man would more heartily have rejoiced than he, to see this cap-stone put by Westcott and Hort upon his building.   The present state of things in England bears testimony, indeed, to Tregelles's labors, but it bears equal testimony to the numbers that, conspicuously or humbly, have entered into those labors. It belongs to all human progress that " one soweth and another reapeth ;" and in this instance, surely, there is abundant cause that " he that soweth and he that reapeth may rejoice together."

[1] Certain early parts of Tregelles's edition of the New Testament are reported by credible witnesses as bearing the imprint of Wiley, New York, and I remember to have seen, a number of years ago, something of the sort myself; but I have not been able lately to obtain information definite enough to warrant further detailed mention.

XI. THE FOREIGN SUPPLY.

EVERY one knows that the American editions by no means comprise the entire supply of Greek Testaments used in this land during the present century. Yet the American editions —especially the non-critical—have had an immense circulation amongst three classes : (1.) Those who have revered the *textus receptus* almost as a matter of religious faith, and have known nothing of its myriad variations. These have been the easiest prey for the vendors of the sham editions. A natural result; but what a commentary upon their ignorant despising of the labors of conscientious critics! (2.) Those who cared little for a critical text, and wished only to have a taste of the original flavor for themselves. (3.) The multitude of students who used the New Testament as one of their early aids in acquiring the Greek language. To these might be added a fourth: those sermonizers who, not very familiar with the Greek Testament, used the cheapest means for " examining critically," as their phrase is, their sermon text, with the help of lexicon, grammar, and our Common English Version. These, of course, were the least excusable and the least profited of all.

But of the foreign editions most current here in the first half of this century, the popular ones would seem to be the various Scotch and English editions based on Mill, the Greek-Latin reprints of Leusden by the Wetsteins and by Wingrave, etc., with the Knapp and Scholz editions. The students had their Valpys, and a few others of note as specimens of voluminous book-making, very much as they now have their Wordsworth. Burton was used a little; and it is within the course of the present generation that Webster and Wilkinson, used a little, gave way to Alford for those who could afford it. The era of general discrimination, in respect to either text or commentary, did not arrive much before the present generation; and those who could and did discriminate, were apt to love the masters of the sixteenth century better than their pigmy followers.

Meanwhile, for popular use, Tischendorf was beginning to eclipse all others, with the rather feeble rivalry of Scrivener. The larger editions of Griesbach, Scholz, Tischendorf, and Tregelles, like their predecessors, Mill, Bengel, Wetstein, have always been within the reach of the better scholars, though their popular circulation was never contemplated.

At present, the popular preference for Scrivener's convenient manual seems to suffer some diminution, owing to the Greek New Testaments edited by Scrivener and Palmer, respectively, exhibiting the readings adopted by the Revisers, and to the "Parallel New Testaments," by the same editors, which exhibit the same Greek text and margins, together with the Common and the Revised English Versions. Popular use seems to demand some edition which will furnish the Greek readings adopted or preferred by the Revisers, and facilitate a comparison between the Common and the Revised Versions. Of the four editions (or rather, five, for Palmer's with the Greek only appears in two forms) just mentioned, Palmer's seems to be everywhere—and naturally—preferred; for its Greek text is that of the Revised Version, with the variants in the margin, while Scrivener's gives generally the Greek text of the Common Version, with the readings of the Revised in the margin.[1]

---

[1] The scholars have the same preference, on additional grounds. Scrivener's presents the text of Beza's folio of 1598, with an Appendix of variations where the Revisers of 1611 appear to have adopted a different text. These variations are those found in other editions of Beza, in the Complutensian, the Aldine, Erasmus, Colinæus, the Latin Vulgate, Tyndale of 1526, and the English of 1611. But he ignores the *minor*, 8vo, editions of Beza, 1565, 1567, 1580, 1590, 1604, which are much nearer the Authorized Version than the folios. If Scrivener had taken these minor editions into consideration (as the Revisers of 1611 must have done), he would perhaps have selected a different edition as the text "more likely than any other to be in the hands of King James's revisers, and to be accepted by them as the best standard within their reach" (*Parallel N. T.*, p. xxiv.; or ed. with Greek text alone, p. vii.). At all events, his Appendix would

But it is quite plain that the choice of the bulk of students, in the matter of a manual, lies between Westcott and Hort,

have had an entirely different complexion, and have shown that where his "B" stands for "all the editions" of Beza, it is oftener in error than not. As it is, his Appendix is not quite free from error on its own basis. (I speak on these points from personal examination, having also in my own library all of the ten editions of Beza except the *minor* ones of 1565 and 1590.)   Further, he adheres to his former error of considering the Greek-Latin New Testament of Barbirius and Courteau (Basil., 1559, 1560; and Tiguri, without publisher's name, 1559) as a Beza edition.   That edition indeed contains Beza's Latin Version, but not his Greek text.   The error had been committed by others before Scrivener (*e. g.* John Leusden, *Philologus Hebr.-Græc.*, p. 62), but it was exposed more than a century ago by Masch (*Biblioth. Sacr.*, Pars I. Cap. II. Sect. II. ₰ XXXV., *Editiones Bezanæ spuriæ ;* compare Pars II. Vol. III. Cap. III. Sect. II. ₰ 16), more recently (1872) by Reuss, and again repeatedly by others since Scrivener fell into it in 1874 (*Plain Introd.*, 2d ed., p. 390).

But the depths of Scrivener's mystification and confusion over the Beza editions are not reached in these works of his that are cited above.   In the third edition (1883) of his *Plain Introduction* (p. 440, notes 1 and 2) sundry positions are taken which are not to be reconciled either with his former positions or with the facts.   He tacitly abandons his former opinion that the Pseudo-Beza of 1559 (also 1560) was Beza's first edition, and takes the edition of 1556 as Beza's first, speaking confidently of its *Greek text.*   But the edition of 1556, as already remarked, contained no Greek text at all.   It was part of Robert Stephens's great folio Latin Bible of 1556–57 (the second whole Latin Bible of his divided into the modern verses) containing the Vulgate and the version of Pagninus in the Old Testament, and the Vulgate and the first edition of Beza's Latin Version and Annotations in the New Testament.   The New Testament title is dated 1556, its colophon 1557; the Old Testament title is dated 1557.   Beza's Latin was not printed with any Greek text till 1559 (in the book above referred to); and that was not Beza's work, but the doing of the enterprising publishers at Basel.   Beza's first Greek text was published in 1565.

Stress is laid by Scrivener, in the notes above cited, upon Beza's own representation of his editions.   But a comparison of Beza's title-pages with his dedications to Queen Elisabeth, in the several folio editions, and with his address to the kind reader in the edition of 1598, shows plainly that Beza's numbering of his editions refers only to his Version and his Annotations.   In fact, it might be urged with plausibility, that a strict grammatical construction of the title of the folio editions of 1565 and 1582, if the punctuation is regarded, confines his numbering to the Annotations alone; and that a more liberal interpretation, especially, in the face of the known facts, could hardly carry it beyond the preceding "altera, noua [interpretatio], Theodori Bezæ, diligenter ab eo recognita." *Litteratim et punctatim*, the title to the 1565 edition (or so much of it as we have here to deal with) runs thus : " IESV CHRISTI D. N. | Nouum testamentum, | *siue Nouum fœdus.* | Cuius Græco textui respondent interpretationes duæ : | vna, vetus: altera, noua, Theodori Bezæ, di- | ligenter ab eo recognita. | *EIVSDEM TH.*

on the one hand, and Von Gebhardt's Tischendorf, on the other. The fact is encouraging, for it shows decidedly the advance of New Testament scholarship, not to say the progress of correct ideas. Westcott and Hort's edition will win and hold its place by sheer merit; but the additional conveniences found in Von Gebhardt (the various readings of Tregelles and of Westcott and Hort, the parallel references,

---

BEZAE ANNOTA- | *tiones, quas itidem hac secunda editione recognouit,* | *& accessione non parua locupletauit."* Now, cheerfully granting that all this is to be construed liberally, as applying to a second edition of Beza's work, it is perfectly consistent with the fact that the Greek text was not in the former edition, to say the least. To be more liberal, and insist that this means a second edition of Beza's Greek text, is to make the man stultify himself. But Beza has not done so. The Dedications to Queen Elisabeth, in the several editions, refer to the earliest edition as if to a Latin version with annotations, only. Thus, in the Dedication in the edition of 1565, Beza says; "Annus iam agitur octauus ex quo nostram hanc noui Testamenti vel potius Fœderis versionem, additis annotationibus, aggressus," and he follows that theme as his main one. Of course Beza's notes of time bring us back to 1556 or 1557 as the date of that first edition—of Latin text and Annotations, which is all there was of it. Nor is there anything in the title (or elsewhere) of the subsequent editions which, read without perversion, is inconsistent with or contradictory to the facts. To lay stress (which I cannot think Dr. Scrivener does) on the phrase "*Græco contextu,*" in his quotation (*idem*) from Beza's edition of 1598, as if it meant a Greek text printed with the Latin one of 1556, would be to claim for Beza an equally early use of the Syriac version (which was first used in the edition of 1582), and to follow a wrong track altogether.

I have looked a little to see if I could find any early authority for this error; but among the older writers I have seen only the following in the second edition (1723, fol.) of Le Long's *Bibliotheca Sacra,* tom. ii. p. 638, in the list of Biblical works by Beza: ^h 7. Annotationes majores in Novum Testamentum unà cum textu Græco & versione sua Latina, in fol. *Genevæ* 1556. 1565. 1582. 1588. 1598." But here the "1556" is an inadvertence merely; for Le Long repeatedly shows that he knew better. He notices no such Greek-Latin book elsewhere, though he several times, in different connections, states that Beza's Latin Version and Annotations were first printed in 1556; besides correctly describing, in proper place, the work in which they are found. Moreover, in describing Beza's Greek-Latin New Testament of 1565, he quotes (verbatim, but not quite literatim) from its title as follows, inserting the parenthesis with italicized words : " Ejusdem Theod. Bezæ annotationes, quas itidem hâc secundâ editione (*prima enim est anni 1556, absque textu Græco*) recognovit, & accessione non parvâ locupletavit." In Le Long's first edition (Antwerp, 1709, 16mo) he has no such error, but gives the descriptions and statements just referred to in about the same words, even to the parenthesis with "*prima enim est anni 1556, absque textu Græco.*"

the "Adnotatio Critica," and the greater ease of finding a place—a matter in which German books surpass so completely the clumsy English, and too often American, contrivances) will make it the favorite of many for habitual use, though they might prefer Westcott and Hort for continuous reading, and for the matter found in the second volume. According to the Rev. Dr. Carl Bertheau of Hamburg, who is no mean authority in such matters, Von Gebhardt's edition is quite an immaculate book in respect to typography. In a communication to the (Leipzig) *Theologische Literaturzeitung* of Harnack and Schürer, 2 December, 1882, pp. 560, 561, after mentioning the correction of an *iota* dropped in some impressions, Bertheau says: "Im übrigen ist uns kein Fehler im Drucke dieser Ausgabe vorgekommen oder sonst bekannt geworden." And he goes on: "Sie wird jetzt . . . als die empfehlenswertheste Handausgabe des *N. T. gr.* zu gelten haben" (he is speaking, however, of editions published in Germany). But no one who knows both Westcott and Hort and Von Gebhardt will be willing to do without either.

The signs of the times, as discerned in the antiquarian bookstores of New York and Philadelphia, are quite suggestive in one respect that should not be passed over. For some months those stores have been unusually well stocked with new copies of the beautiful Oxford Greek Testaments of the common text, for sale at a very low rate. They are also well supplied with the common Cambridge editions of like text; and also with certain books which attempted to float into wide circulation on the tidal-wave of the Revised English Version, but whose lack of requisite scholarship took away their buoyancy, and left them stranded at the price of *five cents a copy*.

Since the Old World must remain the depository of the vast mass of material for restoring the true text of the Greek New Testament, it is hardly to be supposed that America alone, at least for the present, can either do the critical work for the world or supply its critical text. But the day has long gone by of which Dr. Francis Wayland lamented (*Collegiate System in the United States*, p. 129): "We have in this country scarcely anything that can be called a library: the means do not exist among us for writing a book, which in Europe would be called learned." On the whole, the general foreign supply of Greek New Testaments in the first half of this century, and somewhat later (except the larger critical editions and some of the smaller German editions), was little, if at all, better in quality than the home supply. Numerically, the inferior publications prevailed in both England and America; while the representative—at least the book-making—New Testament scholars here were as high in grade and at least as low in prejudice as those of England. American scholars of this century have been neither idle nor unfruitful in their contributions to the common end of New Testament elucidation and critical completeness. Most interesting, were this the appropriate place, would be a sketch in outline of their work of the sort; a work of which the most remarkable item and example is that, now in progress, of two American scholars —Dr. Caspar René Gregory, in Leipzig, and Dr. Ezra Abbot in Cambridge, Massachusetts—engaged in compiling the Prolegomena which Tischendorf's death left wanting to his great critical edition.

But from like or kindred efforts the American scholars, though often working in obscurity, have never improperly hung back; nor are their researches or their results to be ignored at home, any more than in other quarters of the scholarly world.

XII. CHRONOLOGICAL LIST OF GREEK NEW TES-TAMENTS PUBLISHED IN AMERICA.

THIS account would be incomplete without an exhibition of the subject matter in its chronological aspect simply. The following list is intended to include all the issues of the American Greek New Testament, or parts thereof, treated of in the preceding sections. The character of each issue will appear as follows: A * designates a part only of the Greek New Testament. Where the entire item is in brackets, the edition, except sometimes the titlepage, is one actually printed abroad. Where an earlier text or edition is chiefly followed, the earlier name is generally given in parenthesis at the first occurrence of each example.

1800. (Mill.) C. Alexander. Worcester, Thomas, 12.
1806. Leusden, Gr.-Lat. Philadelphia, Bradford, 12.
1806. Leusden. Philadelphia, Bradford, 12.
1809. Griesbach. (3d ed.) [W. Wells.] Cambridge, Wells & Hilliard, 8.
* 1810. (Elzevir.) Macknight, Apostolical Epistles, Gr.-Eng. Boston, Wells, Wait, & Co., 8.
1814. (Mill.) Boston, Thomas, 12.
* 1814. (Griesbach, 3d ed.) Stuart, Newcome's Harmony. Andover, Flagg & Gould, 8.
* 1814. The same, 4.
1821. Leusden, Gr.-Lat. New York, George Long, 12.
1822. (R. Stephanus.) Peter Wilson. Hartford, Cooke, 12.
1822-23. (Griesbach, 3d ed.) Kneeland, Gr.-Eng. Philadelphia, Small, also Fry, 12.
1822. The same, Gr. only, 12.
1823. The same, Gr.-Eng., 12.
1823. The same, Gr. only, 12.
1824. (Wilson.) Pseudo-Leusden, Gr.-Lat. New York, Collins & Hannay, 12.
1825. Wilson. Hartford, Cooke, 12.
* 1825. (Griesbach, 3d ed.) [N. L. Frothingham,] Gospels. Boston, Cummings & Hilliard, 8.

5   65

1827. Wilson. Hartford, Cooke, 12.
1829. Wilson. Hartford, Cooke, 12.
1829. Wilson. Philadelphia, Towar & Hogan, 12.
* 1830. E. Friederici, John, Gr.-Eng. New York, G. F. Bunce, 12.
1831. Wilson. Philadelphia, Towar & Hogan, 12.
1831. Pseudo-Leusden, Gr.-Lat. New York, Collins & Hannay, 12.
. 1833. Wilson. Philadelphia, Towar, Hogan, & Thompson, 12.
* 1834. (Knapp, 4th ed.) Robinson, Newcome's Harmony. Andover, Gould & Newman, 8.
1835. Pseudo-Leusden, Gr.-Lat. New York, B. & S. Collins, 12.
1835. (Knapp, 4th ed.) Patton. New York, Starr, 4.
1835. The same (text printed on one side of the leaf only), 4.
1836. Pseudo-Leusden, Gr.-Lat. New York, Collins, Keese, & Co., and Dean, 12.
1837. Bloomfield (2d Lond. ed.), Stuart. Boston, Perkins & Marvin; Philadelphia, H. Perkins, 8.
1837. The same. Boston, Perkins & Marvin; New York, Gould & Newman; Philadelphia, H. Perkins, 8.
1838. Wilson. Philadelphia, Haswell, Barrington, & Haswell, 12.
1838. Pseudo-Leusden, Gr.-Lat. New York, Collins, Keese, & Co., and Dean, 12.
1838. (Greenfield.) Polymicrian, Engles. Philadelphia, H. Perkins; Boston, Perkins & Marvin, 32.
1839. Polymicrian, Engles. Philadelphia, H. Perkins; Boston, Perkins & Marvin, 32.
1840. Pseudo-Leusden, Gr.-Lat. New York, W. E. Dean, also Collins, 12.
1840. Polymicrian, Engles. Philadelphia, H. Perkins; Boston, Perkins & Marvin, 32.
1841. Polymicrian, Engles. Philadelphia, H. Perkins; Boston, Ives & Dennet, 32.
[1842.] *n. d.* Robinson's Hahn. New York, Leavitt & Allen, 12.
1842. Robinson's Hahn. New York, Leavitt & Trow, 12.
1842. Robinson's Hahn. Boston, Crocker & Brewster, 12.
1843. Bloomfield, 5th Amer. ed. Philadelphia, Perkins & Purves, 8.
1844. Pseudo-Leusden, Gr.-Lat. New York, W. E. Dean, 12.
1844. Polymicrian, Engles. Philadelphia, Perkins & Purves, 32.
1845. Robinson's Hahn. New York, Leavitt & Trow; Boston, Crocker & Brewster, 12.
1845. The same. New York, Leavitt & Trow; Boston, Crocker & Brewster, 8.
1845. Patton. New York, J. C. Riker, 4.
1845. The same, printed on one side of the leaf only, 4.
* 1845. (Hahn.) Robinson's Harmony. Boston, Crocker & Brewster, 8.
1846. Bloomfield, 5th Amer. ed. Philadelphia and Boston, Perkins, 8.
1846. Polymicrian, Engles. Philadelphia, H. Perkins, 32.
1846. Polymicrian, Engles. Philadelphia, Perkins & Purves, 32.
* 1847. (Burton.) Spencer, Gospels and Acts. New York, Harpers, 12.
1847. (Burton.) Spencer. New York, Harpers, 12.

* 1847. (Hahn.) Collectanea Evangelica, N. R. Brooks. Baltimore, Cushing, 16.
* 1847. The same, 2d ed., 16.
  1848. Polymicrian, Engles. Philadelphia, H. Perkins, 32.
  1848. Bloomfield, 5th Amer. ed. Boston, Perkins; Philadelphia, H. Perkins, 8.
  1848. The same. Philadelphia, H. Perkins; Boston, Perkins & Marvin, 8.
  1848. The same. Philadelphia, H. Perkins; Boston, Benjamin Perkins, 8.
  1849. Pseudo-Leusden, Gr.-Lat. New York, W. E. Dean, 12.
* 1849. (Hahn.) Collectanea Evangelica, Brooks, 3d ed. New York, Barnes, 16.
  1850. Polymicrian, Engles. Philadelphia, H. Perkins, 32.
* 1850. (Hahn.) Owen's Acts. New York, Leavitt, 12.
  1851. Pseudo-Leusden, Gr.-Lat. New York, W. E. Dean, 12.
* 1851. Robinson's Harmony. Boston, Crocker, 8.
  1852. Pseudo-Leusden, Gr.-Lat. New York, W. E. Dean, 12.
  1852. Spencer. New York, Harpers, 12.
* 1852. (Hahn.) Turner's Hebrews, Gr.-Eng. New York, Stanford & Swords, 8.
* 1852. Owen's Acts. New York, Leavitt, 12.
  1853. Pseudo-Leusden, Gr.-Lat. New York, W. E. Dean, 12.
  1853. Polymicrian, Engles. Philadelphia, Clark & Hesser, 32.
* 1853. Robinson's Harmony, rev. ed. Boston, Crocker, 8.
* 1853. (Hahn.) Turner's Romans, Gr.-Eng. New York, Stanford & Swords, 8.
 [1854.] *n. d.* Wilson. Philadelphia, Barrington & Haswell, 12.
  1854. Wilson. Philadelphia, Lippincott, Grambo, & Co., 12.
  1854. Bloomfield, 5th ed. Philadelphia, Clark & Hesser, 8.
  1854. The same. Philadelphia, H. C. Peck & Theo. Bliss, 8.
  1854. Polymicrian, Engles. Philadelphia, Clark & Hesser, 32.
  1854. Robinson's Hahn. New York, Leavitt & Allen, 12.
* 1854. (Elzevir.) Strong's Harmony. New York, Riker, 12.
* 1854. The same. New York, Harpers, 12.
* 1854. (Mill.) [John Lillie,] 2 Peter, 1 and 2 John, Judas, and Revelation, Gr.-Eng. New York, American Bible Union, 4.
  1855. Pseudo-Leusden, Gr.-Lat. Philadelphia, Lippincott, Grambo, & Co., 12.
  1855. Polymicrian, Engles. Philadelphia, H. C. Peck & Theo. Bliss, 32.
  1855. Robinson's Hahn. New York, Leavitt & Allen, 12.
* 1855. (Hahn.) Turner's Romans, Gr.-Eng. New York, Stanford & Swords, 8.
* 1855. (Hahn.) Turner's Hebrews, Gr.-Eng. New York, Stanford & Swords, 8.
* 1855. (Mill.) [O. B. Judd,] Matthew, Chapters I., II., & III., Gr.-Eng. New York, Amer. Bible Union, 4.
  1856. Bloomfield. Philadelphia, Lippincott, 8. (Also several editions from this date down to 1868, dates and edition-numbers unknown.)
  1856. Polymicrian, Engles. Philadelphia, H. C. Peck & Theo. Bliss, 32. (Also several editions from this date onward, the several dates unknown.)

* 1856.   Owen's Acts.   New York, Leavitt, 12.
* 1856.   (Hahn.)   Turner's Galatians, Gr.-Eng.   New York, Dana & Co., 8.
* 1856.   (Hahn.)   Turner's Ephesians, Gr.-Eng.   New York, Dana & Co., 8.
* 1856.   (Mill.)   [Morton,] John, Gr.-Eng.   New York, Amer. Bible Union, 4.
* 1856.   (Mill.)   [John Lillie,] 1 and 2 Thessalonians, Gr.-Eng.   New York, Amer. Bible Union, 4.
  1856-63.   (Griesbach, 3d ed.)   B. Wilson, Emphatic Diaglott, Gr.-Eng. Geneva, Illinois, B. Wilson, 12.
  1857.   Robinson's Hahn.   New York, Leavitt & Allen, 12.
* 1857.   Robinson's Harmony.   Boston, Crocker, 8.
* 1857.   (Mill.)   [N. N. Whiting,] Ephesians, Gr.-Eng.   New York, Amer. Bible Union, 4.
* 1857.   (Mill.)   [N. N. Whiting,] Hebrews, Gr.-Eng.   New York, Amer. Bible Union, 4.
  1858.   Wilson.   Philadelphia, Lippincott, 12.
  1858.   Pseudo-Leusden, Gr.-Lat.   Philadelphia, Lippincott, 12.
* 1858.   (Mill.)   [O. B. Judd,] Matthew, Chapters I., II., and III., Gr.-Eng. New York, Amer. Bible Union, 4.
* 1858.   (Mill.)   [Alex. Campbell,] Acts, Gr.-Eng.   New York, Amer. Bible Union, 4.
* 1858.   (Mill.)   [N. N. Whiting,] Mark, Gr.-Eng.   New York, Amer. Bible Union, 4.
  1859.   Wilson.   Philadelphia, Lippincott, 12.
  1859.   Pseudo-Leusden, Gr.-Lat.   Philadelphia, Lippincott, 12.
  1859.   Spencer.   New York, Harpers, 12.
* 1859.   Spencer, Gospels and Acts.   New York, Harpers, 12.
* 1859.   Robinson's Harmony.   Boston, Crocker, 8.
* 1859.   Turner's Romans, Gr.-Eng.   New York, Randolph, 8.
* 1859.   Strong's Harmony.   New York, Harpers, 12.
* 1859.   (Mill.)   [Morton,] John, Gr.-Eng.   New York, Amer. Bible Union, 4.
* 1859.   Alford, Gospels.   New York, Harpers, 8.
  [1859.   (Scholz.)   Critical Gr.-Eng.   New York, Wiley, 16.]
  [1859.   Codex Vaticanus, Mai.   New York, Appleton, 8.]
  1860.   Wilson.   Philadelphia, Lippincott, 12.
  1860.   Pseudo-Leusden, Gr.-Lat.   Philadelphia, Lippincott, 12.
  1860.   Spencer.   New York, Harpers, 12.
* 1860.   (Mill.)   [N. N. Whiting,] Luke, Gr.-Eng.   New York, Amer. Bible Union, 4.
* 1860.   (Mill.)   T. J. Conant, Matthew, Gr.-Eng.   New York, Amer. Bible Union, 4.
* 1860.   (Mill.)   [N. N. Whiting,] 1 and 2 Timothy, and Titus, Gr.-Eng. New York, American Bible Union, 4.
* 1860.   (Mill?)   [H. B. Hackett,] Philemon, Gr.-Eng.   New York, Amer. Bible Union, 4.
* 1860.   [Hackett,] Philemon, Gr.-Eng.   New York, Amer. Bib. Union, small 4.
* 1860.   Ellicott, Galatians.   Andover, Draper, 8.
  [1860.   Cowper, Codex Alexandrinus.   London, Norgate; New York, Westermann, 8.]

* 1861. Gr.-Eng. Various parts previously published, bound up with general title, etc. New York, Amer. Bible Union, 4.
* 1861. (Theile.) Geo. Wm. Heilig, John, Gr.-Eng. Philadelphia, Desilver, 12.
* 1862. Robinson's Harmony. Boston, Crocker, 8.
* 1862. Ellicott, Ephesians. Andover, Draper, 8.
  1863. Pseudo-Leusden, Gr.-Lat. Philadelphia, Lippincott, 12.
* 1863. Ellicott, Ephesians. Andover, Draper, 8.
  1864. (Griesbach, 3d ed.) B. Wilson, Emphatic Diaglott, Gr.-Eng. Geneva, Ill., B. Wilson, 12.
* 1864. (Mill.) [Joh. Lillie,] Ephesians, Gr.-Eng. New York, Amer. Bible Union, 4.
* 1864. (Mill.) [Morton,] John, Gr.-Eng. New York, Amer. Bible Union, 4.
* 1864. Ellicott, Galatians. Andover, Draper, 8.
* 1864. Ellicott, Thessalonians. Andover, Draper, 8.
  1865. Pseudo-Leusden, Gr.-Lat. Philadelphia, Lippincott, 12.
  1865. Spencer. New York, Harpers, 12.
  1865. B. Wilson, Emphatic Diaglott, Gr.-Eng. New York, Fowler & Wells, 12.
* 1865. Robinson's Harmony, Boston, Crocker, 8.
* 1865. Ellicott, Pauline Epistles, whole set. Andover, Draper, 8.
* 1865. Ellicott, Pastoral Epistles. Andover, Draper, 8.
* 1865. Ellicott, Galatians. Andover, Draper, 8.
* 1865. Ellicott, Ephesians. Andover, Draper, 8.
* 1865. Ellicott, Philippians, Colossians, and Philemon. Andover, Draper, 8.
* 1865. Ellicott, Thessalonians. Andover, Draper, 8.
  1866. Robinson's Hahn. New York, Appleton, 12.
  1866. Emphatic Diaglott, Gr.-Eng. New York, Fowler & Wells, 12.
* 1866. [N. N. Whiting,] Mark, Gr.-Eng. New York, Amer. Bible Union, 4.
* 1866. [N. N. Whiting,] Luke, Gr.-Eng. New York, Amer. Bible Union, 4.
* 1866. T. J. Conant, Matthew, Gr.-Eng. New York, Amer. Bible Union, 4.
* 1866. Ellicott, Pastoral Epistles. Andover, Draper, 8.
* 1866. Ellicott, Galatians. Andover, Draper, 8.
* 1866. Ellicott, Ephesians. Andover, Draper, 8.
  1867. Robinson's Hahn. New York, Appleton, 12.
* 1867 (1866). Ellicott, Galatians. Boston, Draper & Halliday, 8.
* 1867 (1866). Ellicott, Ephesians. Boston, Draper & Halliday, 8.
  1868. Bloomfield, 14th Amer. ed. Philadelphia, Lippincott, 8.
  1868. Robinson's Hahn. New York, Appleton, 12.
  1868. Spencer. New York, Harpers, 12.
* 1868. Ellicott, Pauline Epistles, whole set. Andover, Draper, 8.
  [1868. (Scholz.) Critical Gr.-Eng. New York, Wiley, 16.]
  1869. Bloomfield, 14th Amer. ed. Philadelphia, Lippincott, 8.
* 1869. Owen's Acts. New York, Appleton, 12.
  [1869. B. H. Alford (Alford abridged). Philadelphia, Lippincott; London, Rivingtons; Cambridge, Bell, & Co., 12.]
  1870. Wilson. Philadelphia, Claxton, Remsen, & Haffelfinger, 12.
  1870. Pseudo-Leusden, Gr.-Lat. Philadelphia, Lippincott, 12.
  1870. Bloomfield, 14th Amer. ed. Philadelphia, Lippincott, 8.

1870.   Robinson's Hahn. New York, Appleton, 12.
1870.   Emphatic Diaglott, Gr.-Eng. New York, Samuel R. Wells, 12.
* 1870.   Ellicott, Galatians. Andover, Draper, 8.
[1870, etc. Tregelles. London, Bagster; New York, Wiley, 4.] (Wiley's
          imprint does not seem to be found on all the parts.)
1871.   B. Wilson, Emphatic Diaglott, Gr.-Eng. Geneva, Ill., 12.
* 1871.   Ellicott, Epistles, whole set. Andover, Draper, 8.
* 1871.   Ellicott, Philippians, Colossians and Philemon. Andover, Draper, 8.
* 1871.   (Tischendorf.) Gardiner's Harmony. Andover, Draper, 8.
* 1871.   (Hahn.)   Harmonia Evangelica, Brooks.   Philadelphia, Claxton,
          Remsen, & Haffelfinger, 16.
[1871.   Alford, 6th ed.   Boston, Lee & Shepard, 8.]
1872.   Robinson's Hahn. New York, Appleton, 12.
1872.   Emphatic Diaglott, Gr.-Eng. New York, S. R. Wells, 12.
* 1872.   Robinson's Harmony. Boston, Crocker & Brewster, 8.
* 1872.   Gardiner's Harmony. Andover, Draper, 8.
[1872.   Alford, 6th ed.   Boston, Lee & Shepard, 8.]
* 1873.   Gardiner's Harmony. Andover, Draper, 8.
[1873.   Alford, 6th ed.   Boston, Lee & Shepard, 8.]
[1874.   Alford, 7th ed.   Boston, Lee & Shepard, 8.]
1875.   Pseudo-Leusden, Gr.-Lat. Philadelphia, Lippincott, 12.
1875.   Robinson's Hahn. New York, Appleton, 12.
1875.   Spencer. New York, Harpers, 12.
* 1875.   Owen's Acts. New York, Appleton, 12.
* 1875.   Gardiner's Harmony. Andover, Draper, 8.
[1875.   (Scholz.) Critical Gr.-Eng. New York, Wiley, 16.]
[1875.   Alford, 7th ed.   Boston, Lee & Shepard, 8.]
1876.   Pseudo-Leusden, Gr.-Lat. Philadelphia, Lippincott, 12.
1876.   B. Wilson, Emphatic Diaglott, Gr.-Eng. New York, Wells, 12.
* 1876.   Owen's Acts. New York, Appleton, 12.
* 1876.   Gardiner's Harmony. Andover, Draper, 8.
* 1876.   Ellicott, Philippians, Colossians, and Philemon. Andover, Draper, 8.
* 1876.   Ellicott, Thessalonians. Andover, Draper, 8.
* 1876.   Ellicott, Galatians. Andover, Draper, 8.
* 1876.   (Scrivener's R. Stephanus 3d.) Henry A. Buttz, Romans. New
          York, Nelson & Phillips; Cincinnati, Hitchcock & Walden, 8.
1877.   Spencer. New York, Harpers, 12.
* 1877.   Buttz, Romans. New York, Nelson & Phillips, 8.
[1877.   (Scholz.) Critical Gr.-Eng. New York, Wiley, 16.]
[1877.   Alford, 7th ed.   Boston, Lee & Shepard, 8.]
1878.   Pseudo-Leusden, Gr.-Lat. Philadelphia, Lippincott, 12.
* 1878.   Ellicott, Epistles, whole set. Andover, Draper, 8.
* 1878.   B. Wilson, Emphatic Diaglott, Luke. New York, Wells, 12.
[1878.   Alford, "new edition." Boston, Lee & Shepard, 8.]
* 1879.   Robinson's Harmony. Boston, Houghton, Osgood, & Co., 8.
* 1879.   The same. Boston, Houghton, Mifflin, & Co., 8.
* 1879.   Ellicott, Epistles, whole set. Andover, Draper, 8.
* 1879.   Ellicott, Galatians. Andover, Draper, 8.

* 1879. Ellicott, Ephesians. Andover, Draper, 8.
* 1879. Gardiner's Harmony. Andover, Draper, 8.
* 1879. Buttz, Romans. New York, Nelson & Phillips, 8.
* 1879. (Lachmann.) Shedd, Romans. New York, C. Scribner's Sons, 12.
  [1879. (R. Stephanus, 3d ed.) Scrivener. New York, Holt, 16.]
  1880. Wilson. Philadelphia, Claxton, Remsen, and Haffelfinger, 12.
  1880. Pseudo-Leusden, Gr.-Lat. Philadelphia, Lippincott, 12.
  1880. Robinson's Hahn. New York, Appleton, 12.
  1880. B. Wilson, Emphatic Diaglott, Gr.-Eng. New York, Wells, 12.
* 1880. Ellicott, Epistles, whole set. Andover, Draper, 8.
* 1880. Gardiner's Harmony, rev. ed. Andover, Draper, 8.
  [1880. (Scholz.) Critical Gr.-Eng. New York, Wiley, 16.]
  [1880. Alford, "new ed." Boston, Lee & Shepard, 8.]
* 1881. Ellicott, Pastoral Epistles. Andover, Draper, 8.
  [1881. Alford, "new ed." Boston, Lee & Shepard, 8.]
  1881–82. Westcott & Hort (Schaff). New York, Harpers, crown 8.
  1882. Pseudo-Leusden, Gr.-Lat. Philadelphia, Lippincott, 12.
  1882. Westcott & Hort (Schaff), Gr.-Eng. New York, Harpers, 8.
* 1882. Robinson's Harmony. Boston, Houghton, Mifflin, & Co., 8.
* 1882. Owen's Acts. New York, Appleton, 12.
* 1882. Ellicott, Philippians, Colossians, and Philemon. Andover, Draper, 8.
  [1882. (Scholz.) Critical Gr.-Eng. New York, Wiley, 16.]
  1883. Polymicrian, Engles, second edition, Hall. Philadelphia, Perkins, 32.
  [1883. (Scholz.) Critical Gr.-Eng. New York, Wiley, 16.]
  [1883. Alford, new ed. Boston, Lee & Shepard, 8.]

Without date; and not enumerated in the foregoing.

Wilson. Philadelphia, Barrington & Haswell, 12. (An issue with a printer's
  mistake in paging, as early as 1851.)
The same, corrected.
(Greenfield.) Polymicrian, Engles. Philadelphia, Theo. Bliss, 32.
The same. Philadelphia, H. C. Peck & Theo. Bliss, 32.
The same. Philadelphia, Peck & Bliss, 32.
The same. Philadelphia, Lippincott, 32.
Robinson's Hahn. New York, Leavitt & Allen, 12. (With a different street-
  number of the publishers.)
(Knapp, 4th ed.) Patton. New York, Riker, 4.
The same, printed on one side of the leaf only, 4.
* Tafel, Gospels, Acts, and Revelation, Gr.-Eng. Philadelphia, Tafel; Lon-
  don, Nutt, 8.
* The same. New York, E. & J. B. Young; London, James Speiss, 8.
  [(Scholz.) Critical Gr.-Eng. New York, Wiley, 16.]
  [The same. Philadelphia, Lippincott, 16.]
  [The same. London, Bagster; New York, Wiley, 16.]
  [The same. London, Bagster; Philadelphia, Lippincott, 16.]
  [Greenfield, Polymicrian. London, Bagster; New York, Wiley, 32.]
  [The same. London, Bagster; Philadelphia, Lippincott, 32.]

The preceding list comprises 257 items, of which 150 are issues of the entire Greek Testament, and 107 are issues of a part only. Of issues which have escaped my search, whose (probable or) possible existence has been indicated at the appropriate place in the foregoing pages, the number, according to the most reasonably framed conjecture, should be not far from thirty. Forty, in my opinion, would be too many.

As it may be interesting to know how the rate of production has varied, I subjoin a tabulated statement of the numbers which have been issued in each decade. The year given is that of the close of each decade; and the count for each decade is made to the end of that year. The table includes all the editions whose time of issue has been ascertained, whether dated or undated:

Decade Ending:	Entire New Testaments.	Partial Editions.	Total.
1800.	1.	0.	1.
1810.	3.	1.	4.
1820.	1.	2.	3.
1830.	11.	2.	13.
1840.	15.	1.	16.
1850.	21.	6.	27.
1860.	29.	34.	63.
1870.	20.	27.	47.
1880.	26.	28.	54.
1883.	8.	4.	12.
Total,	135.	105.	240.

To these are to be added the remainder, of undated issues whose actual time of publication has not been ascertained. The numbers are as follows: issues of the entire New Testament, 15; of partial editions, 2; total, 17. Editions without date began to be issued in 1842, at the latest, and have been continued nearly, if not quite, to the present time; though their number has been diminishing for the last ten years. The repetitions of these undated issues add, of course, to the absolute number of copies produced in the country; but, except in case they should be found to bear some clear distinguishing mark, they could not with strict propriety be enumerated as distinct issues, even if their number were ascertainable.

A glance at the list will show, better than any summary in

words could do, how the supply has varied from year to year. The years which are not represented in the list are 1801, 1802, 1803, 1804, 1805, 1807, 1808, 1811, 1812, 1813, 1815, 1816, 1817, 1818, 1819, 1820, 1826, 1828, 1832; or, nineteen years out of the eighty-four. The traces left on the list by the political or financial condition of the country are discoverable; but they are not perfectly intelligible and clear without more discussion than is called for in a work of this character; and if not so, the facts might be interpreted differently by different economists. The effect of the war of 1812 is evident at first glance; but that of other momentous events does not generally lie on the surface. An important factor to be considered, also, is the effect of the appearance of an epoch-making edition in Europe; for our scholars and instructors have always kept a sharp lookout for all progress there. Robinson's Hahn, for example, would doubtless have had a much larger and more continued circulation, had it not been for the appearance of Tischendorf's editions. The circulation of the latter has been immense in this country, and that without a single reprint.

The question how far, or how many of, the editions actually printed abroad should find a place in this list, or in a work of this kind, I shall not attempt to raise. The question of production for the market (to take only that view of the matter) is settled independently of the sub-consideration whether it shall be done by importation (of sheets or plates), or by actual manufacture. It is not easy to draw the line between the mere ventures of the foreign publishers, on the one hand, and the enterprise of the native publisher or the judgment of the native scholar, on the other. An attempt to draw the line would often be as unjust, as it would be, in the matter of unquestioned native manufacture, to inquire whether the publisher did his own type-setting or printing, or had it done by other hands, in another establishment, or in another town. The real question, were it worth the raising, and were it to be answered if raised, is really one of principal and agent, in a sense somewhat broader than the legal one. The facts are given, as well as they could be searched out; and their interpretation is left to the reader. Whatever that interpretation may be, it cannot be unfavorable in respect of American fondness for the Greek New Testament. The American consumption, to speak after the manner of the economists, of the home and foreign product, can scarcely fall short of half a million copies; and even that number—enormous as it is, all things considered, in its ratio to the supply of other countries—may be an underestimate.

To attempt particularly and precisely to account for this vast number of Greek New Testaments distributed in America, would be to deal with conjecture only. But it is to be remembered that in the early days of American colleges, and down nearly to the middle of the present century, a knowledge of the Greek Testament was conspicuous among the requirements for entrance; and thus the men of collegiate training became pretty well acquainted with it in their youth. Besides that, the regular Monday morning exercise, for a great part of the college course, was a reading and recitation in the same book; a practice which fell into partial disuse, but is now restored in many institutions. In most of the larger towns in New England, at least, there were a few professional men who kept up its habitual reading, even among the non-church-going inhabitants. In my father's own congregation, as I well remember (his pastorate of twenty-three years ended in 1855; and one of his trials in his subsequent theological professorship of twenty-one years was the lack, on the part of the theological students, of early acquaintance with the Greek Testament, not to mention the superiority which divers of them, like the head of the University of Louvain in the Vicar of Wakefield, felt to the whole subject), not only were there several men of the learned professions who could and did read regularly their Greek Testament, and who were " able to appreciate the broadside force of an argument " whose essence lay in the Greek text, but there was also a small knot of youth—and some of them of the gentler sex—whose knowledge and habits of study put them in a corresponding intelligent position. I think I am not mistaken in believing that in many homes besides that of my own boyhood, the children were taught, not only by precept, but by an example never to be forgotten or to fail in power, that " it is a disgrace to an educated man not to be familiar with his Greek Testament."

INDEX.

ADDENDA.

Since the preceding pages were stereotyped, the following items have come to light:

1848. Robinson's Hahn. New York, Leavitt & Trow; Boston, Crocker & Brewster, 12.

* 1872. Ellicott, Epistles, whole set. Andover, Draper, 8. (Each part has separate title, and the date 1872.)

MONITUM.

The misprint (Jude 25), noted in the facsimile page of Thomas's Greek Testament, does not appear in all the copies.

On page 11, line 3 from bottom, the two Greek words should exchange places.